'Contending for the [faith] that is precisely what [...]

book. He singles out four heretical positions adopted in the early church—Ebionism, Montanism, Arianism and Pelagianism— and shows that they alive and well in modern church life. Even though the old terms may not be used, yet the doctrinal positions are in effect the same. He traces with care the way in which the various views developed, and how they have resurfaced time and again.

This book is a wake-up call to modern Christians, who have often lost the concern for doctrinal accuracy that marked out Christians in other eras. Though dealing with doctrine, it is easy to read, and the reference to modern Christian aberrations should alert a spirit of watchfulness in readers. Many do not realise how easy it is at times to depart from orthodox belief and practice. This book helps us to reassess Christian belief and practice in our own day.

Allan Harman

Christianity and its Competitors delivers more than its title and chapter titles convey. Dr. McGoldrick draws provocative, daring lines from the ancient errors of the Ebionites and Judaizing Christianity, Montanism, Arianism, and Pelagianism to the contemporary errors that plague the theology and/or practical teachings of Roman Catholicism, Mormonism, Socinianism, Unitarianism, Universalism, Arminianism, Semi-Pelagianism, Jehovah's Witnesses, Christian Science, fundamentalism, and various charismatic movements.

Though on a few occasions one may fear that the author draws his lines too confidently, in the main his exposure of ancient and contemporary errors is scriptural, clear-headed, challenging, and makes for a fascinating read.

Joel R. Beeke

Christianity and its Competitors

James Edward McGoldrick

CHRISTIAN FOCUS

Quotations from the Bible are taken from the New King James Version, except where noted.

Copyright © James McGoldrick 2006

ISBN (10) 1-84550-140-3
ISBN (13) 978-1-84550-140-2

Published in 2006
by
Christian Focus Publications, Geanies House,
Fearn, Ross-shire, IV20 1TW, Scotland

www.christianfocus.com

Cover design by Alister MacInnes (info@moose77.com)

Printed and bound by
Norhaven A/S Paperback, Denmark

Contents

Preface

No author is without debtors, so I am pleased to acknowledge the help of the many others who have contributed to my development as a scholar and a writer. Special thanks are due to Dr Alan Lair, who first suggested this project, and to Dr David Ludwick, who read the manuscript and made helpful suggestions of improvement. Dr Joel Beeke too rendered valuable assistance in this regard. The staff at Christian Focus Publications, of course, deserves my gratitude for accepting my work and editing it with much care.

James Edward McGoldrick
Taylors, South Carolina
2006

Introduction

Although Christianity in its numerous expressions comprises the most populous religion on earth, its competitors are many, and some of them have displayed terrific energy in recent years. Among the millions of people who claim allegiance to the Christian faith, there is a bewildering diversity of belief and practice, and the lack of fundamental agreement among them has encouraged the growth of competing systems of belief. Like many other terms, the word *Christian* requires careful definition, lest an indistinct use of the designation leads to misunderstanding. In the religious climate of the early twenty-first century, there is a tendency to regard as Christian any school of thought which professes allegiance to the teachings of Christ, no matter how vaguely it may do so. Such allegiance is often only traditional or perfunctory and does not indicate fidelity and devotion to Jesus Christ as the New Testament describes his person, his doctrines, and his work. Since this is so, the competitors of Christianity are not only those religions which reject the claims of Christ, but those which assume the prerogative of diluting his teachings or choosing from among them the ones which to them appear attractive.

The Apostle Paul, as he closed his ministry in Ephesus, told the elders of the church there, "I have not shunned to declare to you the whole counsel of God" (Acts 20:27). That commitment to affirm and assert the message of Christ in its entirety has motivated the writing of *Christianity and its Competitors*. This book is not a dispassionate examination of various opinions regarding the Christian faith. It is rather a vigorous assertion and defense of Christian belief by an author whose confidence in the trustworthiness of the Bible is without reservations.

The procedure in this study is to examine some of the major challenges to biblical belief which appeared in early Christian centuries and then to relate how such teachings gained acceptance and have continued to confront the faith in modern times, even though modifications have occurred and groups which espouse them no longer bear the names of the ones which promoted them during the era of the ancient church. A careful comparison of ancient heresies with the major doctrines of the current competitors will show that to "contend earnestly for the faith which was once for all delivered to the saints" (Jude 3) remains a matter of urgency for the Church of Jesus Christ.

In dealing with matters of controversy, as this book does, it is appropriate for the author to identify his doctrinal position at the outset. It is well to affirm allegiance to the authority of Scripture, but because disagreements about the meaning of Scripture are common an exact statement is in order. My persuasion is that of historic Reformed theology, as expressed in the Westminster Confession of Faith and the Larger and Shorter Catechisms. This subscription includes my endorsement of such ancient declarations of faith as the Apostles' Creed and the Creed of Nicea. While the supreme authority of the Bible must take precedence over every ecclesiastical effort to summarize and publish Christian doctrines, I believe that the creeds of the ancient church and the confessions of the Protestant Reformation have done so accurately and are therefore reliable subordinate expressions of God's revealed truth. This being so, references to these documents will appear throughout this study.

In evaluating challenges to historic, orthodox teachings which comprise the subject matter of this book, two principal considerations have formed the analysis and determined the judgments rendered. The critical examination of each ancient heresy and its modern counterpart addresses first, the question of the authority for faith, and second, the teaching of a particular religious body with regard to the person of Christ. In those cases where a sect denies the sole authority of Scripture and the eternal essential deity of Christ, this study considers it a pseudo-Christian cult. Some of the religious movements under consideration here have committed only one of these errors, and in those cases the judgment is less assertive. In this frame of reference, it is necessary to distinguish between errant Christians and cults which have no legitimate claim to being Christian. This should avoid unfair and needlessly divisive assessments, and to the best of my ability I have observed this caution. If I have failed to do justice to a particular religious group, I apologize and entreat correction. Although many scholars have contributed to my understanding and have influenced my views, the verdicts I have rendered are entirely my own, for which I alone must bear responsibility. May the Triune God, who is the Author of all Holy Scripture, use this volume for the instruction and edification of all who read it.

Chapter One

Ancient Heresy:
Ebionites and Judaizing Christianity

Origins Within the New Testament Era

The Jewish roots of the Christian faith are obvious, but the church quickly became a predominantly Gentile movement. The public perception for much of the first century was that Christianity was a sect of Judaism comparable to the Pharisees, the Sadducees, or the monastic Essenes. The Roman imperial government at first considered the new faith as a school of Jewish thought, and accordingly Rome granted the church the status of *religio licita* – a legal religion. The apostles and other church leaders portrayed Jesus as the fulfillment of Old Testament prophecies, and the Bible of the Hebrews became the Sacred Scriptures for Christians. For several decades after the crucifixion of Jesus, the Romans allowed Christians to operate as a division of Judaism under the protection of imperial law.

The Christians themselves did not renounce their Jewish

heritage, and the Apostle Paul emphatically declared his Jewish identity by insisting he was "of the tribe of Benjamin, a Hebrew of the Hebrews; concerning the law, a Pharisee" (Phil. 3:5). As a missionary Paul's procedure was to seek fellow Jews and to proclaim Jesus to them as their long-awaited Messiah (Christ). Prior to Paul's embrace of the Christian faith, Peter and other disciples had urged Jews to realize "that God has made this Jesus, whom you crucified, both Lord and Christ" (Acts 2:36).

The first generation of Christians was composed almost entirely of ethnic Jews, who, as believers in Jesus, assumed that the Savior's work was for Israel alone. Should Gentiles desire to become Christians, they would have to become proselytes to Judaism first. That is, converts from paganism would have to submit to the laws of Judaism in addition to receiving Christ through faith. One faction within the church, for example, insisted "unless you are circumcised according to the custom of Moses, you cannot be saved" (Acts 15:1).

The Apostolic Response to this Crisis

The apostolic response to this demand came primarily from Paul, who encountered a party of *Judaizers* that scorned his message of salvation for Jews and Gentiles by grace alone, through faith alone, in Christ alone. This legalistic view of Christianity threatened to undermine the basis of salvation, even as it disrupted the unity of the church. If the teaching of the Judaizers had prevailed the church would have become in fact one more sect of Judaism, as the Romans already regarded it. The crisis was of such magnitude that church leaders gathered in Jerusalem in *c.*AD 48 in order to resolve the matter.

At the council in Jerusalem, the apostles and elders

listened to Peter report about his ministry among Gentiles. He informed the assembly that Gentile believers, like their Jewish-Christian brethren, had received the gift of the Holy Spirit, and "God made no distinction between us and them, purifying their hearts by faith" (Acts 15:9). Paul and Barnabas, his missionary companion, reinforced Peter's report by informing the church leaders that God had blessed their preaching to the Gentiles and had ratified it by performing "many miracles and wonders...among the Gentiles" (Acts 15:12). These appeals persuaded the assembly to reject the Judaizing doctrine and to affirm the acceptance of gentile believers on the same basis as believing Jews. The church then was to have no national or ethnic identity (Acts 15:22-29; cf. Ephesians 3:1-7). Jesus Christ is the Savior of the world, so his spiritual body is universal in its constituency.

The Spread of the Judaizing Teaching

The decision at Jerusalem was a monumental event, but the doctrine it rejected continued to spread. A short time after the council, perhaps as early as AD 49, Paul confronted that teaching in Galatia, a region in Asia Minor, where the population was predominantly Gentile. He wrote his Epistle to the Galatians, which is a systematic rebuttal of the Judaizers' doctrine and a manifesto of the gospel of salvation *sola gratia* – by grace alone.

The Apostle Paul believed that genuine Christianity would not endure were the Judaizing heresy to triumph, so he wrote a confrontational letter to the churches of Galatia in which he denounced the harmful falsehood then circulating among them. He concluded that those who were promoting it "pervert the gospel of Christ" (Gal. 1:7). He accused his opponents of proclaiming "a different gospel" (Gal. 1:6), one without saving power. The Apostle cited Abraham as an Old Testament example of one saved by grace alone and justified (declared righteous) through faith alone, "for Abraham believed God, and it was accounted to him for righteousness" (Gal. 3:6). Paul then applied that truth to the Galatian situation, when he wrote:

> *therefore know that only those who are of faith are sons of Abraham, and the Scripture, forseeing that God would justify the Gentiles by faith, preached the gospel to Abraham beforehand, saying, 'in you all the nations shall be blessed. So then, those who are of faith are blessed with believing Abraham' (Gal. 3:7-9).*

Since God's acceptance of Abraham preceded the patriarch's circumcision, that ceremonial rite could not have been the basis. Abraham

> *received the sign of circumcision, a seal of the righteousness of the faith which he had while still uncircumcised, that he might be the father of all those who believe, that righteousness might be imputed to them also (Rom. 4:11).*

When Judaizers demanded that Gentile believers in Christ submit to circumcision and to the ceremonial laws of Judaism, Paul concluded that they were imposing a "yoke of slavery" upon such converts (Gal. 5:1). Circumcision could not and did not save anyone in the Old Testament. In the New Testament it has no moral or spiritual value, "for in Christ Jesus neither circumcision nor uncircumcision avails anything, but faith working through love" (Gal. 5:6).

When the council at Jerusalem issued its pronouncement about the status of Gentile converts, it reflected the teaching of the Old Testament itself, which had promised the inclusion of Gentiles within God's covenant community. Peter, as recorded in Acts 15:15-19, referred to the prophecy of Amos 9:11-12, which cites the inclusion of Gentiles as part of God's plan. Isaiah too was specific in relating that the Servant of Jehovah would be a "light for the Gentiles, that you [the Servant-Messiah] may bring my salvation to the ends of the earth" (Is. 49:6, NIV), and Simeon took Jesus in his arms and hailed him as "a light to bring revelation to the Gentiles, and the glory of your [God's] people Israel" (Luke 2:32).

Although the New Testament affirms that God does not recognize any religious distinction between Jewish and Gentile believers (Eph. 3:1-6), the Judaizing teaching persisted, and some of its concepts have never ceased to attract acceptance. Jewish opposition to Christians in the Roman Empire led eventually to persecution of Christians for which militant Jews were responsible. Stephen became the first Christian martyr of record, and his enemies stoned him because, they said, he had spoken "blasphemous words against Moses and God" (Acts 6:11). It appears ironic that people who claimed to be Christians would oppose the Apostolic teachings and resist those who proclaimed them, but that is exactly what occurred. Judaizing teachers were known to follow Paul and other missionaries for the purpose of undermining their authority and leading their converts away from the gospel of salvation by grace alone. This happened, for example, in Antioch, when "certain men came down from Judea and taught the brethren, 'unless you are circumcised according to the custom of Moses, you cannot be saved'" (Acts 15:1).

The Jewish Revolt Against the Romans

The Apostle Paul, the major object of the Judaizers' wrath, died in Rome before AD 64, and in AD 66 Jews in Palestine revolted against the imperial authorities at a time when

Jewish nationalism was at a fever pitch. The uprising initiated four years of bitter warfare which devastated the Jews and led to the destruction of Jerusalem in the year 70. Christians did not support the revolt, but the Romans continued to view them as Jews. As a consequence, Christianity lost its status as a tolerated religion and became *religio illicita,* an illegal religion subject to imperial repression. Occasional persecutions of Christians occurred until the early fourth century, when Emperor Constantine (r. 306-37) declared himself a believer in Christ.

During the struggle against the Romans, many Jews and Christians fled from Jerusalem, and the Judaizers were among them. Post-Apostolic Christian authors sometimes referred to these Judaizers as *Ebionites*, the transliteration of an Aramaic term which means poor. The significance of such a designation for this sect is not clear. Among the Jewish monks at Qumran, near the Dead Sea, it was a term of honor, and some early Christians thought it a desirable word for identifying true disciples of Jesus, the Lord who was very poor while upon earth (Matt. 8:20). Irenaeus (*c.* 115-202), Bishop of Lyons in Gaul, appears to have been the first church leader to identify a sect by the name of Ebionites. He indicated that its adherents regarded the Apostle Paul as a traitor who had scorned divine law. The Ebionites presented the gospel as a new law and insisted upon circumcision and other ceremonies of Judaism. The sect possessed a version of the Gospel of Matthew in Hebrew, perhaps a corrupted text, which has not survived. The Ebionites maintained that the entire law of Moses would remain binding for all time. Since Paul taught otherwise, his writings were false. One view of Paul, held within this sect, considered him a pagan who had embraced Judaism for base reasons. Paul defended himself vigorously against similar charges, as his statement in Philippians 3:1-6 attests.

The distinctives of Ebionite teaching included rejection of the essential, eternal deity of Christ. Although the sect acknowledged Jesus as the Messiah, it asserted an adoptionist view of his person. According to this doctrine, God the Father adopted Jesus as his son when John baptized Jesus in the River Jordan. This belief entailed rejection of Christ's virgin conception and miraculous birth. Jesus then was reduced to being a reformer who purged Judaism of false accretions such as the requirements for animal sacrifices. [1]

As Ebionites understood the work of Christ, his death had nothing to do with salvation, which is the reward for human works of merit. Jesus was a prophet who taught the correct meaning and proper application of the divine law in the manner of the prophets in the Old Testament.

Although there was strong opposition to Ebionite teachings in Christian circles, the sect enjoyed considerable numerical strength as an organized religious body for several centuries. Mosaic laws of purification regulated the lives of the members, and poverty they regarded as a great virtue. Ebionites claimed to preserve true Christianity, as it had been before Paul's influence had corrupted it. They thought they had incorporated the best features of Judaism and Christianity, but the traditional Jews considered them a fraud, and the Christians viewed them as heretics. The Ebionite movement plagued the church for the first four centuries but declined in the fifth century. Remnants survived in Egypt and Jordan until Islam engulfed those countries in the seventh century.

The Modern Counterpart: Religious Legalism

Salvation Through Ceremonies

The Ebionites' emphasis upon ceremonies and adherence to Old Testament ceremonial laws exerted its greatest initial influence in the Eastern Mediterranean region, but the belief that true religion consists in the proper performance of prescribed rituals became popular in Western Europe as well. As the Middle Ages progressed, at both Constantinople and Rome, the church gradually elaborated its services of worship until they became intricate, ornate rituals in which every gesture had religious significance and was believed to be essential. To omit a prescribed gesture or even to alter it was intolerable. A graphic example of this thinking occurred in Russia, to which Byzantine missionaries had taken the faith in the tenth century, the first churches being formed in Kiev, now the capital of Ukraine.

The introduction of Christianity into the Kievan principality occurred during the reign of Vladimir I (r. 978-1015), and from the beginning the ruler dominated the church. This practice continued down the centuries, and after the Grand Duchy of Moscovy gained control over most of the country, in the sixteenth century, it became common for Christians to refer to their homeland as Holy Russia. Clergymen told their mostly illiterate congregations that Russian piety was Christianity in its purest expression. The state protected the church, and the priests reciprocated by affirming the divine-right of the autocracy. Russian religious leaders did not foresee that the loss of all ecclesiastical autonomy and absorption into the machinery of state institutions lay ahead.

The spiritual character of the Russian Church was very weak, and the immutable sacred liturgy was, in popular belief, the essence of Christianity. Every letter and dot in traditional religious texts was regarded as holy, and the church viewed its ceremonies as divinely ordained and therefore unchangeable. Russian religion was a

> set form of prayer formulas, possessing a magic meaning, and the slightest detail, eliminated or changed, deprived the formula of that mysterious force in which he [the Russian church member] believed without questioning its origin.[2]

In 1453 Constantinople fell to the Ottoman Turks, and the Greek Orthodox Church became subject to the new Muslim rulers. Some Russian churchmen contended that this was a divine judgment on the Greek Church because it had sought reunion with the papacy, from which it had been separate since the schism of 1054.

The Russian Orthodox Church obtained its religious texts and its ceremonies from Byzantium, and the Russian clergy had transmitted them over the centuries. Most Russian priests were ignorant, and some were illiterate. The low level of learning among them left them unable to detect gradual corruptions of their sacred texts which were due to copyists' errors or to mistakes in translations from Greek into Church Slavonic. When some scholars displayed discrepancies between the Russian documents and those of the Greeks, Russian priests complained that the Greeks had deviated from the original faith, and the Russian versions were the standards of real orthodoxy.

The controversy about the correct liturgical texts erupted in part because Tsar Basil III (r. 1505-33) ordered translation of some religious books into Slavonic, and Maxim the Greek (c. 1470-1556), a learned monk from Mt. Athos, arrived in Moscovy in 1517 to undertake the task and to correct some errors in the Russian materials. Despite the tsar's support for the project, the reaction of the church hierarchy was one of outrage. Metropolitan Bishop Daniel of Moscow led the attack upon Maxim and other scholars engaged in textual criticism, and as a result Maxim and his associates spent several years in an ecclesiastical prison after being condemned for heresy and black magic.[3]

As bizarre as the Maxim case was, it was not a singular instance of ecclesiastical intolerance. Before the sixteenth century ended, a bitter dispute arose about the proper way to make the sign of the cross. The Russian custom was to do so with two fingers, but the Greeks used three. Some Russian clergymen contended that the Greek practice implied a denial of the two natures of Christ. In a similar dispute the Russians insisted that religious processions must follow the sun and not walk toward it, for to walk into the sun was tantamount to refusing to follow the steps of Jesus.[4]

As Christianity spread across Western Europe, the Latin Church, rather than the Greek, came to dominate the landscape. The Latin Church, too, slowly became rigorously ceremonial in its worship, although it did not manifest as much rigidity as the Eastern churches were doing. In the West the church maintained a large degree of independence from civil authorities after the Roman Empire collapsed in 476. In principle the Latin Church had never submitted to the Roman state, even after the empire became officially Christian by edict of Theodosius I (r. 379-95). In fact, as the Middle Ages unfolded, it became clear that some of the more ambitious popes aspired to reduce civil rulers to obedience to Rome. Perhaps one such effort occurred when Pope Leo III (r. 795-816) crowned Charlemagne, King of the Franks (r. 768-814), as Emperor of the Romans on Christmas Day in the year 800. Whatever dignity the Frankish ruler gained by this bestowment, it is evident that the pope needed a powerful protector against the depredations of his Italian enemies.

Although Charlemagne considered himself a loyal churchman, his support of the papacy was not one of subservience. The Frankish ruler had his own political agenda, and he cleverly perceived that he could pursue it while aiding Rome at the same time. Franco-papal co-operation conveyed the impression that the church and state were united in a mutual effort to advance the Kingdom of God. Charlemagne believed, for example, his brutal conquest of pagan tribes, in which he forced them to be baptized and to espouse Christianity, was an appropriate expression of his faith and devotion to the church.

During Charlemagne's reign, compulsion in matters of religion became common. He supported the hierarchy's demand for uniform patterns of prayer, and he required all parents to have their children baptized in order to cleanse them from original sin. This monarch enforced canon laws relating to church attendance, fasting, etc. He decreed death for people who ate meat during Lent and for those who cremated the dead. By insisting upon uniform ceremonies, the king and his bishops promoted developments in doctrine and practice that led the church ever farther from its biblical foundations. Preaching declined in quality and frequency, as liturgical formalities became central in services of worship. Often priests read sermons which had survived from early church Fathers, but many priests did not preach at all. By this time the transition from the New Testament faith to formal medieval religion was far advanced. Theologically and in practice, the clergy had become a professional elite of necessary mediators with God, and the veneration of departed saints had acquired cultic status. Fear of ecclesiastical authorities and their civil accomplices made most people docile servants of the church.[5]

The Changing Concept of Priesthood

Underlying the movement away from the New Testament simplicity there was an unbiblical and therefore harmful belief about the priesthood; one that developed gradually until the clerical establishment assumed commanding influence in the church. The office of priest, obviously, is one of divine ordination, and during the era of the Old Testament specific biblical injunctions regulated admission to the priesthood and stipulated the functions of priests and provided means to support them. Their very existence attested to the need for mediators with God, that is, an order of divine servants to represent the covenant community in worship, and in atoning for sin through required sacrifices.

The New Testament preserved the office of elder and prophet, but it does not affirm a continuing professional priesthood from Old Covenant times. Even the Apostles, Christ's hand-picked leaders of the church, do not appear as priests in the New Testament record, except as they participated in the priesthood which is common to all believers (I Pet. 2:9). It is important to note that although the Apostles were the Savior's closest companions, recipients of direct revelation, and, in some cases, authors of Holy Scripture, they did not refer to themselves as priests, nor did they award that office to any other leaders in the church. Peter, the most prominent of the original twelve Apostles, in writing to "the pilgrims of the Dispersion," identified himself carefully by asserting, "the elders who are among you I exhort, I who am a *fellow elder*" (I Pet. 5:1, emphasis mine).

Peter and other authors of the New Testament did not regard themselves as professional priests because they understood that the Old Testament priesthood was no longer in effect. Jesus Christ had fulfilled all the proper functions of the priesthood and is now the sole "mediator between God and men" and the perfect sacrifice for sin which Old Testament priestly sacrifices prefigured (I Tim. 2:5-6; John 14:6). The exclusive and final priesthood of Christ is an emphatic teaching of the Epistle to the Hebrews, which extols the Savior's finished work of atonement for the salvation of his people (Heb. 7:20-28). The imperfect priesthood of the Old Testament with its repeated sacrifices has ceased because Christ, the perfect high priest, "has appeared to put away sin by the sacrifice of himself" (Heb. 9:26).

Despite the clear and insistent teaching of the New Testament, however, a body of professional mediator-priests developed in the church and became larger and more powerful. As a consequence, an ecclesiastical hierarchy arose which perpetuated features of the Jewish priesthood, which the work of Christ had rendered no longer valid. Clergymen dressed in distinctive religious garb comparable to priests of Judaism. They collected tithes from the laity and created levels or graduations of honor and authority among themselves. In this way the office of bishop achieved a dignity far greater than that of an ordinary pastor, and archbishops became the equivalent of princes ruling over provinces of the church; whereas Jesus had directed the Apostles to regard themselves as *servants* of God's people, and he set an example for them by coming to earth "to serve and to give his life a ransom for many" (Matt. 20:25-28). Many professional priests, on the contrary, like the Lord's ambitious disciples, were concerned primarily to gain positions of influence and power (Mark 9:33-37).

Congruent with the heavily ceremonial character of worship services and the dominance of the clergy, the church of late antiquity and the Middle Ages assumed the right to impose elaborate and intricate requirements upon its members, and for many such obligations there was no biblical warrant. Relatively few people could read the Scriptures, and copies were scarce, so laymen were forced to depend upon the priests to represent them before God. Obedience to the established church and its priesthood was the paramount duty of every professing believer, even though ordinary pastors often were barely literate and did not consider teaching the doctrines of the faith as part of their clerical function. Priests and parishioners often thought that being a Christian meant fulfilling the ceremonial duties that the church prescribed, so a theology of salvation by works of merit eclipsed the gospel of grace. The church did not teach that people could save themselves, nor did it deny the necessity for saving grace. It did, however, maintain that grace alone (*sola gratia*) will not bring salvation. The role of grace, as most medieval teachers understood and declared it, is to impart an ability to perform works of righteousness and thereby to obtain the reward of eternal life. Grace plus works then leads to salvation. *Synergism*, the belief that salvation is a co-operative endeavor to which God and humans contribute, became and remains the most popular view of salvation in the Roman Catholic Church. Sincere but poorly informed church members relied on their priests to dispense the grace of God, and they believed that their own deeds would determine where they would spend eternity. In popular thinking, human merit was central and God's grace peripheral. The Catholic Church of the Middle Ages, by exalting the clergy inordinately and by imposing non-biblical requirements for salvation thereby, perpetuated the teaching of the Judaizers in the form of religious legalism.

Current Forms of Legalism

In the teaching of the Roman Catholic Church and the Eastern Orthodox churches, the primacy of the professional priesthood remains undiminished. *The Twentieth Century Encyclopedia of Catholicism*, for example, describes a priest as "another Christ," as it explains his role in the eucharist:

> *The priest who gives thanks and consecrates does not do so in his own name nor even as representative of the community; he represents the Christ of the Supper; he repeats his actions; he is his image, his visible and living image.*[6]

An equally explicit and even more recent declaration appears in the *Catechism of the Catholic Church*, a 1994 publication, which bears the stamp of Vatican approval.

> *It is the same priest, Christ Jesus, whose sacred person his minister truly represents. Now the minister [priest] by reason of the sacerdotal [priestly] consecration which he has received, is truly made like to the high priest and possesses the authority to act in the power and the place of the person Christ himself.*[7]

Although the Roman Church affirms the supreme priesthood of Christ and a priesthood of believers, it maintains that the benefits of Christ's sacrifice become effective through the sacrament of the eucharist performed by a professional priest. Laymen enjoy the privileges of priesthood because the clergy officiate in dispensing the grace of God.[8] In doing this the clergy enable laymen to perform the works of merit necessary for salvation. An infusion of grace empowers believers to seek God; it makes them " capable of acting as his children and of *meriting* eternal life."[9] In explaining grace, the *Catechism of the Catholic Church* indicates that it is an unmerited gift from God, and

> *moved by the Holy Spirit and by charity, we [believers] can then merit for ourselves and for others the graces needed for our sanctification, for the increase of grace and charity, and for the attainment of eternal life.*[10]

By insisting that the priests of the hierarchy are necessary mediators of grace, and by imposing a requirement for human merit as part of the basis for acceptance with God, the Roman Church perpetuates the doctrine of the Ebionites. Romanism then is one form of legalism in that it goes beyond Scripture in demanding from sinful human beings merit that God does not require for salvation.

Belief in salvation as a reward for human endeavors continues to be popular, especially among people who understand religion to be the proper performance of prescribed rituals. Those who espouse such views always deny the inherent sinfulness of human nature, for to admit the reality of human depravity would negate the possibility that sinners could make any meritorious contribution to salvation. The idea that sinners can earn merit with God is a form of religious humanism. The message of Christ's gospel is that salvation is a free, unmerited gift from God bestowed upon all who embrace Christ through faith and repent of their sins (Eph. 2:1-10; Titus 2:3-8). Humanism assumes that, despite their sinful condition, people possess the ability to please God and to fulfill the requirements of his law. Scripture, however, asserts emphatically, in the words of Paul:

> *we know that whatever the law says, it says to those who are under the law, so that every mouth may be silenced and the whole world held*

accountable to God. Therefore no one will be declared righteous in his sight by observing the law; rather through the law we become conscious of sin. . . . We maintain that a man is justified [declared righteous] through faith apart from observing the law (Rom. 3:19-20, 28 NIV).

According to the Bible, salvation is not a matter of what people do for God, but a matter of what God does for them. Any teaching that attributes salvation to man is a form of legalism comparable to the doctrine of the ancient Judaizers.

Although religious doctrines which promote salvation through ceremonies and/or human works of merit are the most conspicuous expressions of legalism, there are other modes of that falsehood deserving of attention. Among them is one that enjoys broad acceptance with some conservative Protestants known commonly as fundamentalists. Such Christians are fervent defenders of the Bible, and they profess to adhere to its supreme authority over all areas of doctrine and life. Very often, however, some of them define Christian piety or spirituality in terms of adherence to extra-biblical requirements. It is ironic that people disposed to this are among the most vehement critics of the Roman Catholic Church because of that body's denial of *sola scriptura* – the authority of Scripture alone.

In fundamentalist congregations there is, for example, in general a demand for total abstinence from alcoholic beverages, even though Scripture does not mandate it. Church members who fail to abstain sometimes incur the charge that they are sinning, and persistence in the practice could lead to church discipline. Drunkenness is not the issue, for the biblical condemnation of that is obvious – no "drunkard will inherit the Kingdom of God" (I Cor. 6:10). Prohibitions against theater attendance and dancing are other items often on the fundamentalists' agenda. Those people who engage in such activities are, in the eyes of some legalists, terribly deficient in spirituality, if they are Christians at all.

Demanding fidelity to non-biblical standards for the regulation of behavior, when appraised scripturally, must be rejected as egregious error, one which Jesus forcefully condemned. Matthew 15:1-20 reveals the Lord's disdain for legalism. He was engaged in a dispute with the scribes and Pharisees, who were self-appointed guardians of rabbinical teachings. Some of those teachings bore little or no resemblance to divine laws, but the rabbis insisted upon them nevertheless. The Jewish leaders asked Jesus, "Why do your disciples transgress the tradition of the elders? For they do not wash their hands when they eat bread" (15:2). The Savior retorted quickly, "Why do you transgress the commandment of God because of your tradition?" (15:3). The contention had nothing to do with hygiene. It pertained to a ceremonial washing which the rabbis demanded on their own authority.

Jesus proceeded to indict his critics on another point – they implemented a rabbinical interpretation that allowed people to evade the responsibility of caring for their needy parents. They could invoke the law of *corban* (Mark 7:11), which would permit them to declare their assets dedicated to God and therefore not accessible for aiding their parents. This enactment not only lacked biblical basis, it violated the specific commandment "honor your father and your mother" (Ex. 20:12). Jesus then scorned the contentions of the legalists by concluding:

> These people honor me with their lips, but their hearts are far from me. They worship me in vain; their teachings are but rules taught by men (Matt. 15:8-9, NIV).

In rebuking the adherents to rabbinical tradition, Jesus cited Scripture, in this case Isaiah 29:13. In Christ's view, his dispute with the scribes and Pharisees was a collision between opposing religions, one rooted in tradition, the other in God's Word. In other terms, it was an argument between *legality*, as God ordained it, and *legalism*, as the Jewish leaders conceived it. There was an impasse between biblical and extra-biblical authorities, and Jesus accused his opponents of rejecting the divine law. As he expressed it, "you nullify the Word of God for the sake of your tradition" (Matt. 15:6, NIV).

To engage in legalism by imposing requirements God has not mandated is to deny the sufficiency of Scripture. Divine revelation, not human preferences, must be the standard of judgment. As the Westminster Confession of Faith states precisely:

> the whole counsel of God concerning all things necessary for his own glory, man's salvation, faith and life, is either expressly set down in Scripture, or by good and necessary consequence may be deduced from Scripture: unto which nothing at any time is to be added, whether by new revelations of the Spirit or by traditions of men (I, vi).

Sola scriptura was the formal principle of the Protestant Reformation, but many heirs of the reformers have lapsed into the errors of the Pharisees and their rabbinical mentors by insisting upon compliance with non-biblical, and, in some cases, anti-biblical requirements. Christians must uphold the permanent authority of God's moral law in Scripture, and there is no place for lawless behavior in Christians' lives. The assertion of the Apostle Paul, "the law is holy, and the commandment holy, just, and good" (Rom. 7:12) must be the conviction of all of Christ's disciples in all ages. That law remains God's standard for holiness, and it provides a sufficient monitor by which to appraise true spirituality. A godly person will concur with King David, who wrote, "his delight is in the law of the Lord, and in his law he meditates day and night" (Ps. 1:2).

Since salvation is *sola gratia,* by grace alone, the law is not and could not be the means by which sinners obtain acceptance with God. God's moral law exposes human failure and condemns sinners who violate its prescriptions and prohibitions. It pronounces "all the world...guilty before God" (Rom. 3:19). This law is flawless because it comes from the perfect God, who demands perfect obedience, as Jesus said, "you shall be perfect, just as your Father in heaven is perfect" (Matt. 5:48). The grace of God brings forgiveness and salvation to believing penitent sinners through the redeeming work of Jesus Christ, and people who receive this grace thereafter love God's law and submit to it eagerly as they meditate upon it (Ps. 119:97). They need no other standard than the divine revelation of Scripture, which they regard as sufficient for "doctrine, for reproof, for correction, for instruction in righteousness, that the man of God may be complete, thoroughly equipped for every good work" (2 Tim. 3:16-17). To resort to extra-biblical sources for ascertaining God's will for Christian living is to impugn the authority and sufficiency of God's written Word, even God himself, as ancient Judaizers and their modern counterparts have done.[11]

Notes

[1] Clear and cogent descriptions of this sect appear in F. F. Bruce, *The Spreading Flame: The Rise and Progress of Christianity from its First Beginnings to the Conversion of the English* (Grand Rapids: William B. Eerdmans Publishing Company, 1958), pp. 279-82 and Philip Schaff, *History of the Christian Church,* II (Grand Rapids: William B. Eerdmans Publishing Company, 1976 reprint of 1910 edition), pp. 428-44.

[2] Paul Miliukov, *Religion and the Church in Russia* (New York: A. S. Barnes & Company, 1942), p. 28.

[3] For a concise account of these strange events, see Michael T. Florinsky, *Russia: a*

History and Interpretation, I (New York: Macmillan Company, 1953), p. 173-75 and Dimitry V. Pospielovsky, *The Orthodox Church in the History of Russia* (Crestwood, NY: St. Vladimir's Seminary Press, 1998), p. 64-65.

[4] Miliukov, *Religion and Church*, p. 29.

[5] Succinct coverage of this era may be found in M. A. Smith, *The Church under Siege* (Downers Grove, IL: Intervarsity Press, 1976), p. 237-49.

[6] Joseph Lecuyer, *What is a Priest?*, tr. Lancelot C. Sheppard, volume 53 of *The Twentieth Century Encyclopedia of Catholicism* (New York: Hawthorn Books, 1959), p. 10. This is an authoritative modern statement of Roman Catholic doctrine.

[7] *Catechism of the Catholic Church*, quoting Pope Pius XII (New York: Doubleday Image Books, 1995), #1548.

[8] iIbid., #1545, 1546, 1547.

[9] ibid., #1813 (emphasis mine).

[10] ibid., #2009, 2010 (emphasis in text).

[11] Joseph A. Pipa, Jr. and J. Andrew Wortman, eds., *Written for our Instruction: The Sufficiency of Scripture for all of Life* (Taylors, SC: Southern Presbyterian Press, 2001), is a collection of perceptive essays which examine this subject and suggest ways to apply the principle. See too O. Palmer Robertson, *The Final Word* (Edinburgh: The Banner of Truth Trust, 1993).

Chapter Two

ANCIENT HERESY: MONTANISM

The End of the Apostolic Age

By the latter half of the second Christian century, the absence of the New Testament Apostles began to have a telling effect upon the churches. To some extent the fervor and devotion of Christians in the first century was diminishing, and some people lamented that condition. They tried to revive the church by claiming that God was still at work in miraculous ways, even as he had been when the Apostles were present to lead the church. The intentions of such people were noble, but they committed a serious error in that they failed to recognize that the age of special revelation and miraculous gifts of the Holy Spirit ended with the passing of the Apostles.

In the region of Phrygia in Asia Minor, a movement known as Montanism arose to protest what its teachers perceived to be the decline of spirituality among believers. Montanus, a former pagan priest, professed the Christian faith, and soon after his "conversion" he claimed to have received direct revelation from the Holy Spirit which conferred the gift of prophecy upon him. From this perspective he soon disputed the mediated authority of church leaders, calling for the practice of ecstatic rites in which he purported to be the mouthpiece of God's Spirit. He did not, like the Old Testament prophets, profess to speak for God but insisted that God spoke through him directly. Montanus quickly gained followers, among them Priscilla and Maximilla, who also claimed the gift of prophecy. These women, who left their husbands to follow Montanus, then began proclaiming new revelations.

Claims of the Montanists

Montanus and his two prophetesses, much in the manner of modern Charismatics, insisted that the age of miracles had not ended. That claim caused much excitement and enabled them to influence substantial numbers of people. Montanus himself announced that he was God's instrument of continuing revelation, comparable to a stringed instrument upon which the Holy Spirit played. He maintained that he was under the Spirit's control, a passive channel through which the Word of God flowed, as it had in the ministry of the New Testament Apostles. According to a report from the ancient church historian Eusebius of Caesarea (c. 260-c. 340), the worship services of the Montanists featured intense emotion in which the leader, Montanus,

> was carried away in spirit and wrought up into a certain kind of frenzy, . . . raving and speaking strange things and proclaiming what was contrary to the institutions that had prevailed in the church, as handed down . . . from earliest times.[1]

Montanus claimed the gift of prophecy, which he, Priscilla, and Maximilla possessed, fulfilled Christ's promise that his disciples would do greater things than he had done, after the Paraclete (the Holy Spirit) came to abide with them (John 14:12-18). In Montanus' understanding, the fullness of the Holy Spirit did not occur in the New Testament era but became reality only in his own ministry.[2] The founder of this sect did not encourage all of his followers to prophesy, but he did expect them to accept the divine authority of all pronouncements coming from their leaders. Refusal to do so was to sin against the Holy Spirit.

There was, as could be expected, opposition to the dogmatic assertions of the Montanist prophets, and some members of the movement in Asia Minor abandoned it. Churches in that region divided in their reaction to it. Thyatira remained a stronghold of the sect for about a century.

Montanus and his female associates contended that the gift of prophecy is a permanent endowment that God conferred upon his church until the end of history. Eusebius reported that some zealots of the cult said that Montanus regarded himself as the Paraclete, but evidence for that is not conclusive. It is clear, however, Montanus, Priscilla, and Maximilla considered themselves the last of the prophets, after whose work Christ would return.[3] The ancient theologian Hippolytus (d. c. 180), a contemporary of the Montanist leaders, related that the sect held its female leaders in such esteem that the members "magnify these wretched women above the Apostles and every gift of grace, so that some of them presume to assert that there is in them a something superior to Christ."[4]

Maximilla in particular claimed to be the last of the prophets, the herald of Jesus' imminent advent. She predicted wars and persecutions of Christians would follow her death (which occurred in 180) and precede the coming of Christ. Instead of suffering, however, thirteen years of peace ensued. Contrary to her assertion, more Montanist prophets appeared within twenty years after she died. Their inspiration infused new energy into the sect, and it spread into Egypt.

In accord with their eschatological expectations, Montanists relied heavily upon the Apocalypse, especially upon Jesus' letter to the Church at Philadelphia (Rev. 3:7-13), an epistle which promises Christ's return and the descent of New Jerusalem from heaven. Some members of the sect expected the city from heaven to appear at Pepuza, near Philadelphia in Asia Minor. There is some evidence that they urged all believers to assemble at Pepuza to await that event.[5]

The Role of Tertullian

Although ancient authors such as Eusebius and Hippolytus were hostile toward Montanism, one very distinguished church leader supported the movement and eventually joined it. He was Tertullian (c. 160-c. 225), a lawyer from Carthage, practicing in Rome. Fluent in both Latin and Greek, Tertullian was learned in history and philosophy as well as law. His conversion from paganism occurred about 195, when he began a thorough study of the literature of Christianity. He eventually returned to North Africa to become an elder in the church at Carthage, where he remained until his death.

Tertullian was a committed Catholic Christian, but his understanding of the faith was severely ascetic and somewhat puritanical. He therefore became alarmed by the lax morals and low level of zeal he witnessed among fellow professing Christians. When Roman Emperor Septimius Severus (r. 193-211) initiated persecution against Christians in North Africa,

Tertullian was distressed that many Catholics compromised with paganism in order to evade suffering. His disgust with that cowardice led him to consider the claims of the Montanists in about 206.

Tertullian employed his great scholarship in defending Christianity against attacks from pagan teachers. Being the first Christian theologian to write in the Latin language, historians often cite him as the father of Latin dogmatics. A gifted author, his volatile temper led him to espouse strong opinions. When he thought truth was at stake, Tertullian was uncompromising.

Montanist ideas began to appear in Tertullian's writings by 206, and he had become a prominent member of the sect by 212. His prestige as a scholar made him Montanism's most influential spokesman and gave the movement a respectability and attractiveness it otherwise would not have enjoyed. Montanism provided Tertullian with a vehicle by which to promote his stern, morally demanding version of Christianity, which was perhaps a reaction against the immorality which he had practiced while still a pagan.[6]

It is important to note here that Montanism originated in Phrygia, where its founder functioned as a pagan priest. For some time before the advent of Christianity, that part of Asia Minor had been a center for the worship of Cybele, the Syrian Mother Goddess. That cult featured ecstatic rites, including frenzied dances and self-mutilations by the devotees. This sect was one of the mystery religions which abounded in the Roman Empire during the century before the birth of Christ, and the Montanists appear to have absorbed influences from pagan Phrygia. Examples of this are the prominence of women leaders and a heavy emphasis upon ecstatic ceremonies, which included speaking in strange tongues.[7]

By the time Tertullian embraced their doctrines, Montanus, Priscilla, and Maximilla had been dead for many years, but it is evident that he regarded the teachings of the prophets as revelations from the Holy Spirit. To support his belief in ongoing special revelation, Tertullian described the visionary experience of a female Montanist teacher.

> *Seeing that we acknowledge charismata, or gifts, we too have merited the attainment of the prophetic gift....We have now among us a sister whose lot it has been to be favored with sundry gifts of revelation, which she experiences in the Spirit by ecstatic vision amid the sacred rites of the Lord's Day in the church; she converses with angels and sometimes with the Lord; she both sees and hears mysterious communication; some men's hearts she understands, and to them who are in need she distributes remedies. Whether it be in the reading of the Scriptures, or in the chanting of Psalms, or in the preaching of sermons, or in the offering up of prayers, in all these religious services matter and opportunity are afforded her of seeing visions.* [8]

This description of a charismatic Montanist assembly comes from a source whose support for the sect is undeniable. Tertullian not only promoted Montanism in North Africa, but tried to persuade Callixtus, Bishop of Rome (217-22), to endorse it. For that purpose he went to Rome and gained some influence with the bishop. Perhaps his journey was an effort to purify the Catholic Church at the seat of its most prestigious bishopric. The most vigorous opponent of Montanism at Rome was Praxeas, a theologian from Asia Minor, who succeeded in convincing the bishop and his advisors to reject Montanist teachings, a decision which, in Tertullian's judgment, was the devil's work. [9]

Schism in the Church

Tertullian affirmed all cardinal teachings of the Catholic

Church, and for a long time he cherished the hope that a reform of that church in accord with Montanist beliefs would occur. When that proved to be an impossible dream, he and his fellow sectarians organized their own church with episcopal government, a church in which the office of prophet was the most exalted order of clergy. The close resemblance between the Catholic Church and its Montanist rival is perhaps one reason why the sect did not long endure in Western Europe. In Phrygia it survived much longer, perhaps by emphasizing its differences with the older Catholic body,[10] and by denouncing the Catholic Church as corrupt. Montanists claimed it had lost the inspiration of the Holy Spirit, whose gift of prophecy God had passed to the sect.

It is important to recognize that Catholicism has never denied the possibility of direct, subjective revelation, a fact well attested by the current popularity of charismatic activities within it. In the ancient church, however, the leaders disapproved of the ecstatic experiences Montanists claimed to have enjoyed. The rigorous asceticism of the cult also proved offensive. It is evident that the Bishop of Rome and the Catholic Church in general objected not so much to the principle of continuing special revelation as to the strange practices that belief had generated, especially in Asia Minor. Challenges from the Montanists and other sects encouraged the Catholic Church to solidify its structure of authority through its episcopate.

A major error of the Montanists was their teaching that salvation requires an ascetic style of life. They often complained about the worldliness of many professing Christians, and they proposed legalistic self-denial and renunciation of the world as the means by which to attain to true holiness. The term *asceticism* comes from the Greek *askesis* — "training, discipline, renunciation." In church history it has often meant imitating the example of Christ as the way to salvation. Through its insistence upon asceticism, Montanism encouraged the development of the monastic movement in which monks and nuns acquired recognition as heroic Christians who lived on a superior level of spirituality to which lay people could not attain. A pronounced sacred-secular, clergy-laity dichotomy became characteristic of the medieval church, and that division remains in many Christian denominations. Montanists urged their people to accept martyrdom gladly, even to court it and not evade persecution. Jesus, on the contrary, said, "when they persecute you in this city, flee to another" (Matt. 10:23).

The Modern Counterpart: New Revelations

The Question of Authority

Underlying every question pertaining to humanity's proper relationship with God is the matter of authority. What standard of judgment must people employ to discern truth from error, right from wrong? Christianity has always replied that divine revelation is the only reliable criterion in these matters. Roman Catholic, Eastern Orthodox, and all historic Protestant churches agree. They disagree sharply, however, about how to define revelation. Is the Scripture the sole repository of special revelation (sola scriptura), or are there other channels through which God discloses his will? Sola scriptura, the formal principle of the Reformation, is the Protestant belief: the churches of the Reformation always place their creedal and confessional statements in subordination to Scripture. The Roman Catholic Church and the Eastern Orthodox churches, on the other hand, regard Scripture and ecclesiastical tradition as correlative authorities. In fact, the Greek Orthodox Church considers Scripture to be the first portion of tradition, to which it adds the writings of ancient Church Fathers and the decrees of ecumenical councils of the church.[11]

As the above analysis of Montanism has shown, resort to extra-biblical means of ascertaining the divine will has a long history, and the position of the Catholic and Orthodox churches shows that it continues to command broad acceptance. Among modern cults, which claim to be Christian while yet denying one or more doctrines of the true faith, reliance upon sources of revelation apart from or in addition to the Bible is common.

The Roman Catholic Church is the largest ecclesiastical body that affirms the Christian faith, so its position merits careful attention. Since the Roman Church upholds the essential, eternal deity of Christ, it is not in error on that indispensable doctrine. Regarding the matter of authority, however, the papal church, as do various pseudo-Christian cults, rejects *sola scriptura*, assuming the prerogative of an infallible interpreter of Scripture. *The Catechism of the Catholic Church* explains this in some detail. It begins with a clear declaration that Jesus Christ is the living Word of God, the supreme revelation of the Godhead. "In him he [God] has said everything; there will be no other word than this one."[12] To support this assertion, the catechism cites Hebrews 1:1-2 and quotes a statement from St. John of the Cross (1542-91), a Spanish mystic who believed that, through his contemplations, he received revelations from God. The writings of John of the Cross contain some startling discrepancies which, on the surface, appear to be contradictions. On the one hand, he declared the sufficiency of Christ as God's last Word to humanity. On the other hand, he professed to receive extra-biblical communications from heaven.

John and the church which regards him as an authoritative teacher have attempted to resolve this problem by distinguishing between *public* and *private* revelations.[13] The catechism declares "no new *public* revelation is to be expected before the glorious manifestation of our Lord Jesus Christ."[14] It then hastens to add:

> *Throughout the ages there have been so-called 'private' revelations, some of which have been recognized by the authority of the Church. . . . It is not their role to improve or complete Christ's definitive revelation, but to help live more fully by it in a certain period of history. Guided by the magisterium of the Church, the sensus fidelium knows how to discern . . . in these revelations whatever constitutes an authentic call of Christ or his saints to the Church.*[15]

The correct interpretation and application of such private revelations belongs to "the bishops in communion with the successor of Peter, the Bishop of Rome."[16] Since such mystical experiences are, in the teaching of the Roman Church, actual revelations, it is clear that the papal church does not espouse the sole authority of Scripture. It, on the contrary, frankly denies it. As the catechism states, "sacred Tradition, Sacred Scripture, and the Magisterium of the Church are so connected . . . that one of them cannot stand without the others."[17] "Sacred Tradition and Sacred Scripture make up a single deposit of the Word of God."[18] Perhaps it is noteworthy that tradition precedes Scripture in this assertion, and the catechism identifies tradition as the Word of God. The priority of tradition is apparent in the catechetical admonition to recognize that Scripture

> *is written principally in the Church's heart rather than in documents and records, for the Church carries in her tradition the living memorial of God's Word, and it is the Holy Spirit who gives her the spiritual interpretation of Scripture.*[19]

Although the Roman Catholic Church may be orthodox in its teaching about the person of Christ, and about many other doctrines, it errs seriously by imposing non-biblical requirements for salvation in the manner of the Judaizers, and by elevating its traditions to a level equal with, or even superior to, Holy Scripture. The gravity of these fallacies warrants the inclusion of that church among the competitors of Christianity. Further examination of the Roman Catholic teaching about divine revelation is in the concluding chapter.

Current Charismatic Movements

The most conspicuous expression of belief in extra-biblical revelation among professing Christians occurs in the many Pentecostal-charismatic churches which now command a large following cutting across traditional denominational lines. Since the Church of Rome has from her inception allowed for the possibility of direct inspiration of believers, it should surprise no one that a strong charismatic movement is active within that body and that it enjoys the approval of the hierarchy.[20]

While most observers cite speaking in ecstatic tongues as the major distinctive of charismatic practice, the basis of that movement is a more fundamental consideration. As such this consideration links modern Pentecostals with the Montanist doctrine the ancient church condemned. It is the claim that special revelation did not cease with the end of the apostolic age and the completion of the New Testament. People who espouse this premise are charismatics, whether they do or do not speak in tongues. There would be no reason to speak in tongues were this exercise not believed to be a means to acquire specific directions from God, either public revelations for a church body, or private ones for the benefit of individuals. In fact, the Roman Church is the largest charismatic denomination, even though only a minority of its members claims to speak in tongues.

Charismatics value emotional experience over methodical study, thereby emphasizing what they *feel* more than what they *think*. Perhaps that is why they have produced few theologians and learned Bible scholars. It is common for them to cite Scripture in support of their emotional experiences rather that to examine those experiences critically in the light of biblical teachings. Sometimes charismatics regard their dreams as revelations, and pastors of their churches expound and apply the contents of such dreams rather than preaching from the Bible.[21] A more graphic rejection of *sola scriptura* would be difficult to find among people who consider themselves evangelicals. Since they assume that special revelation is still occurring, they must believe the means of the divine disclosure remains in effect.

Oral Roberts

On occasion Charismatic leaders have become highly controversial, in part, because of the nature of their claims to receive specific communications from God. Oral Roberts (1918-), well-known television evangelist and founder of a university in Tulsa, OK, which bears his name, once announced that he had experienced a vision of Christ, who appeared as 900 feet tall.

Roberts' conversion occurred in 1935, and he reported receiving miraculous healing from tuberculosis very soon thereafter. He became an evangelist and pastor in the Pentecostal Holiness denomination, where his father was already a minister.

In 1957 Roberts initiated traveling tent meeting services under the auspices of his own evangelistic association. Successful use of television soon enabled him to become famous. When the popularity of his healing meetings began to decline, he turned to other avenues for his ministry. Oral Roberts University opened in 1965, and in 1968 he discontinued evangelistic crusades. On television Roberts broadcast prime-time special programs on which he presented celebrities from the entertainment world. By then he had joined the United Methodist Church, and he no longer conducted his work in the style of a Pentecostal Holiness preacher, and in an effort to obtain greater acceptance among traditional churches, he appealed to the mainline denominations to support his expanding programs.

Maintaining Oral Roberts University was an enormous expense, especially after the addition of graduate programs, a medical school, and a hospital named the City of Faith. Although the estimated value of his operations ran into the hundreds of millions of dollars, Roberts eventually overextended his ministries, and serious financial trouble confronted him. He had claimed that God told him to build the City of Faith and to include a twenty-story research tower, where doctors and scientists would produce a cure for cancer. In a letter to supporters the evangelist asserted that he conversed with Jesus for seven hours, and the Lord instructed him to ask each contributor for $240.[22]

Roberts' method of dealing with his financial crisis brought terrific criticism, even from other charismatic leaders. The event that was most damaging to Oral Roberts' reputation was his announcement that God had told him to raise $8,000,000 or he would die. The money was to keep the City of Faith operating. For three months in 1987 Roberts prayed while waiting for donations. Only three hours before God's announced deadline, the owner of a dog racetrack gave him $1,300,000, and God spared his life. The evangelist did not comment about this again until 1995, when he published *Expect a Miracle: My Life and Ministry*. By then City of Faith had closed. There is no evidence that the miraculous cures he promised actually occurred, and cancer remains a killer disease.

Many aspects of Roberts' career seem bizarre, even to people of his charismatic persuasion. He claimed nothing less than divine authorization for what he did, even to the point that he said he had raised the dead.[23] Since he did not accept the sole authority of Scripture, he could not justify his rather strange claims and actions by asserting that he was enacting the will of God communicated to him directly. Since no one else participated in his supposed revelatory experiences, there was no way to verify them.

Roberts made his view of revelation clear in an article entitled "Why Miracles Are for Today." He contended that, without miracles, Christianity would fail to accomplish its mission.[24] Like the prophets of Montanism, Oral Roberts claimed the gift of prophecy, but some of his most spectacular predictions failed. Scripture pronounces a damning indictment upon such "prophets." Deuteronomy 18:22 declares:

> when a prophet speaks in the name of the Lord, if the thing does not happen or come to pass, that is the thing which the Lord has not spoken; the prophet has spoken it presumptuously; you shall not be afraid of him.

Believers in *sola scriptura* must conclude that Oral Roberts is a false prophet.

Pat Robertson

Another prominent television evangelist claiming direct divine inspiration is Marion Gordon "Pat" Robertson (1930-), son of United States Senator A. Willis Robertson (D-VA). Pat Robertson graduated with high honors from Washington and Lee University in 1950 and, after brief service in the Marine Corps, went to law school at Yale University from which he received a degree in 1955. Despite his high intelligence and fine education, he failed to pass the bar examination in New York and did not become a practicing attorney. It appears that, in his early adulthood, Robertson lacked a sense of purpose. While he was at Washington and Lee University, a friend observed that Pat was more interested in parties and girls than in his studies. Heavy drinking and carousing were his pleasure, both as an undergraduate and in law school.[25]

Robertson, while still a boy, had joined a Southern Baptist Church, but he later admitted that he had done so for social rather than spiritual reasons. His mother, however, was serious about her Christian faith, and she never tired of bearing witness to her wayward son and praying for his conversion. To her delight, that occurred in 1956 through the effort of Cornelius Vanderbreggen, a vigorous evangelist, who met Pat in Philadelphia at a time when Robertson was discouraged by lack of success in business and had begun reading the Bible. While Vanderbreggen spoke with him in a restaurant, Robertson experienced what he perceived to be a spiritual rebirth and embraced Christ as his Savior.

When Pat told his Roman Catholic wife Dede about his conversion, her initial reaction was one of skepticism, but soon she witnessed major changes in her husband's life, especially his new concern for others, which became evident when he sold their possessions and gave the money to charity.

49

Robertson was visibly a different man, but his donations to charity sometimes left his family without adequate funds. Not to be deterred by want, he enrolled at the Biblical Seminary (later renamed New York Theological Seminary), and while a student, he became involved in charismatic practices, of which he became a leading proponent.[26] His leadership in the Pentecostal-charismatic movement was dynamic and influential to the point that traditional denominations as well as evangelical church bodies became receptive to its ideas.

Despite meager resources, after graduating from seminary, Robertson bought a television station in Norfolk, VA. Part of his income came from a temporary pastoral position in a Southern Baptist Church.

As a charismatic believer, Pat Robertson was convinced that he enjoyed direct communication with God, so much so that he often claimed divine direction for his actions. Funding his Christian Broadcasting Network, for example, seemed to confirm this belief. In 1963 he organized the now famous 700 Club, a group of that many supporters who pledged $10 per month. The great success of this encouraged expansion of the television outreach, as funds became available through telethon broadcasts. Some viewers reported that miracles occurred as they watched the programs. By 1975 the 700 Club was a nation-wide broadcast and reaching several foreign countries as well. By then the Christian Broadcasting Network had moved to Virginia Beach, where Robertson established a graduate level university.

The nomination of Jimmy Carter for president on the Democratic ticket in 1976 aroused Robertson's desire to put his faith to work in politics. Since Carter made a strong Christian profession of faith, Pat believed the opportunity for a powerful revival of Christianity in public life had arrived.

His television network subsequently produced *It's Time to Pray America*, with charismatic and evangelical leaders such as Chuck Colson, Billy Graham, Pat Boone, Bill Bright, and Rex Humbard participating.

In 1980 Pat Robertson joined with other religious leaders to hold a "Washington for Jesus" rally in the nation's capital, an event that drew at least 200,000 people. Some non-charismatics such as D. James Kennedy, Presbyterian pastor from Coral Ridge, FL, and Baptist pastor Charles Stanley of Atlanta participated. Robertson and Bill Bright of Campus Crusade for Christ were co-chairmen. The size of the crowd made a deep impression upon Robertson, who later expressed delight that it was a multi-ethnic gathering and that Roman Catholics, Episcopalians, Baptists, Lutherans, and others joined in a massive display of Christian unity.[28] At the same time that his Christian Broadcasting Network was expanding and the Washington rally attracted so much attention, charismatic churches were growing in size and in numbers. During the rally several people suggested that Robertson be persuaded to run for president, but his satisfaction with the administration of Ronald Reagan deterred him from entering politics officially. After the re-election of Reagan in 1984, however, Pat declared he would consider seeking the Republican nomination to succeed Reagan. In September 1986 Robertson announced in Philadelphia his intention to seek the nomination, if three million voters signed petitions and promised to work, pray, and contribute to a campaign. As support became evident, he said, "I have walked with the Lord for more than twenty-five years. I know his voice. I know this is his direction. I *know this is his will for my life*."[29] He based his decision on what he perceived to be special revelation from God, and he regarded the three million signatures as signs of divine approval.

Although he enjoyed some initial successes in campaigning, the evangelist could not sustain his momentum with Republican voters, and he withdrew from the race prior to the Republican convention. He has not since sought public office, although he sometimes issues political pronouncements and appraises the performance of people who are in office.

The charismatic complexion of Pat Robertson's political outlook became evident in an interview he granted to *US News and World Report* on February 22 1988. Journalist David Frost asked the evangelist about specific divine instructions as guidance for Robertson's decisions. Frost wanted to know how he could be sure he heard the voice of God and was not listening to his own ideas. Here is Robertson's reply:

> nobody really knows for sure, it's [like] an intimacy between a man and a wife over the years; you [sic] just begin to sense each other's moods and feelings, and you believe you know what it is that your partner for life desires. And a lot of time so-called non-verbal transmittal takes place between two people...Well, it's much the same with God and his people.[30]

Pat Robertson told the interviewer that God had responded to his prayer in miraculous ways on numerous occasions, and blunting the strength of a hurricane in 1986 was a graphic example. In that case the storm was moving toward Virginia Beach, and the full impact threatened to cause much loss of life and colossal damage, even to the Christian Broadcast Network facilities. The evangelist asked God to divert the hurricane out to sea, and that is exactly what happened. The most remarkable aspect of the matter is that Robertson, in the name of Jesus, had commanded the storm to change course. In his words, "it was, of course, a miracle. There's no other explanation."[31]

Often during his telecasts Pat Robertson prays for the cure of people seriously ill. Before a large audience he claimed that healings occurred even while people watched the program. He asserts that God has given him a "word of knowledge," enabling him to know about the particular health problems of his viewers, so he can pray for divine healing. According to associates who work closely with him, such miraculous events happen often.[32]

Pat Robertson's claims are not as audacious as those of Oral Roberts, and his organization has demonstrated fiscal responsibility. His university enjoys considerable respect in the academic world, even its law school, to which Oral Roberts University contributed its law library valued at $10,000,000.[33]

Pat Robertson believes in the cardinal principles of orthodox Christianity, even though he has shown little interest in the teachings of any denomination. Precise definitions of doctrine in the manner of historic confessional churches he does not deem important. Robertson has served in Southern Baptist, Methodist, and Presbyterian churches at various times, and he readily accepts support from people all across the spectrum of Christian beliefs. Like other charismatics, he assigns more value to religious experience than to Scripture, although he and they insist that their practices accord with biblical teaching. Robertson purports to be a defender of biblical Christianity, while at the same time he denies the sufficiency of Scripture by seeking and encouraging resort to extra-biblical revelations in the manner of the ancient Montanists. He provides no objective criteria by which anyone could ascertain whether or not these supposed modern revelations and miracles are actual occurrences of divine intervention. Robertson expects people to accept his judgment about such matters even without verification. Does this position differ in any substantial way from the posture of the papacy?

Jim Jones

Although the errors of charismatic leaders such as Oral Roberts and Pat Robertson are serious, other claimants to extra-biblical revelation have taken this premise to far more harmful ends. One such figure was Jim Jones (1931-78), a native of Lynn, IN, a village near Indianapolis. His father, James Thurmond Jones, a member of the Ku Klux Klan, died while Jim was a boy. His mother Lynetta Jones was a mystic who believed she had communication with her own deceased mother. A "revelation" informed her she would have a son who would lead the world to righteousness. James Warren Jones was the son she expected to be a messiah.

Jim Jones attended a Methodist church and seems to have made a profession of faith in response to the witness of a Nazarene neighbor. He showed much interest in religion as a child and often played church with friends. After graduating from high school, he attended Indiana University but discontinued his studies and began preaching at age eighteen. Still sensing his need for more education, after ten years of part-time attendance, Jones received a bachelor's degree from Butler University in Indianapolis. In 1953 he became pastor of a Methodist church, but some of the congregation resisted his efforts to bring black people into the church, while others objected to his Pentecostal beliefs and practices.

After leaving his Methodist ministry, due to perplexity about his church, Jones organized his own congregation, and in 1956 he founded the People's Temple and soon had a building that had once been a synagogue. To raise funds for the purchase of that building Jones sold monkeys as pets. His racially integrated congregation engaged heartily in Pentecostal-style services. Soon after situating his ministry in the former synagogue Jones and some followers attended a spiritualist meeting, and after that experience Jones professed a belief in reincarnation, and some of the people of the spiritualist persuasion began attending People's Temple.

In 1961 Jim took some youths from his church to Philadelphia to visit Father Divine, a black cult leader who claimed to be God, a claim Jones was willing to acknowledge in some sense of deity. Jones thereafter courted approval from Father Divine, and after the Philadelphia leader died, Jones cultivated his widow Mother Divine, but without success. He said the time had come that he should assume leadership of Divine's Peace Mission, since he and the deceased Father preached the same message of brotherhood and racial reconciliation. As Jones addressed the Peace Mission, he offended Mother Divine by disparaging remarks about the opulence of her facilities in a former luxury hotel. Jones invited the people of the Peace Mission to unite with him in order to pursue "the true apostolic socialism that Father Divine taught."[34] Mother Divine was furious and told Jones and his followers to leave. They did, and about a dozen Peace Mission members went with them. After the experience in Philadelphia, Jim told his disciples to address him as "Father." He contended that Mother Divine rejected his proposed merger because he had refused to have sex with her.[35]

About the time of his failure in Philadelphia, Jim Jones made it known that he denied the virgin birth of Christ, and he summoned his people to give his own pronouncements priority over the teachings of the Bible. He referred to

Scripture as a "black idol." Thereafter he often assailed what he called contradictions and discrepancies in the Bible, while presenting his own prophecies as products of direct special revelation. One of the frequent themes of his preaching was the warning that a nuclear war was coming soon, and only a few places on earth would be safe when it occurred. At one point he took his family to Brazil in search of such a haven, and in 1963 he visited Guyana, which would become the site of a commune to which he wanted his followers to migrate.

Although Jones had been preaching since he was a teenager, he did not obtain ordination as a minister until 1964, when he applied to the Disciples of Christ, a liberal, ecumenical denomination. A committee from that church examined him, and there was concern about his lack of theological education as well as his emotional conception of Christianity. Ordination took place nevertheless, even though Jones by then had become skeptical of historic biblical teachings. The Disciples of Christ have no confessional position, and their constitution then contained no procedure for expelling congregations, no matter what they did.

In 1965 Jones and about one hundred fifty followers settled in Redwood Valley near Ukiah, CA. There the self-acclaimed prophet denounced the Bible, even spat upon it and trampled it under foot. He called Jesus a bastard and his mother Mary a harlot. In hymn singing he directed people to remove the name of Jesus and to insert his own name in place of it. [36] By this time Jones was implying that he was God. He stated explicitly that he was the reincarnation of Jesus, the Buddha, Bab of the Bahai Faith, and Vladimir Lenin, the first Soviet dictator. He informed his followers that most of them had known him in a previous incarnation. [37] According to a defector from the cult, Jones "was openly bragging that he was God Almighty by the time the San Francisco temple was ready for use as a worship center."[38]

Jim Jones was a charismatic in that he claimed to exercise miraculous powers (*charismata*), and he exemplified the popular usage of that term in his ability to impress people inside and outside of his sect with his personal magnetism. In 1961 Mayor Charles H. Bowell of Indianapolis made Jim director of Municipal[?] Rights Commission in recognition of Jones' work to promote racial equality. The opening of the People's Temple in San Francisco and Los Angeles in 1971 enabled him to become a potent political figure in California, where he gained fame for his anti-drug efforts, establishing clinics and nursing homes, for which he received public funds. By 1975 Jones controlled enough votes to assure the election of George Moscone as Mayor of San Francisco. The mayor reciprocated by appointing Jim as the chairman of the city's Housing Authority. Moscone sometimes addressed the congregation at People's Temple, and on occasions other politicians appeared there and with Jones at other public gatherings. Even Governor Jerry Brown and Vice-Presidential candidate Walter Mondale sought his support. When Jimmy Carter was seeking the presidency, his wife Rosalyn enlisted Jones to hold a rally for Carter, and she later ate with him.

The news media did not pay much attention to Jim Jones until he demonstrated ability to influence political affairs. By late 1976 some investigative reporters began to examine People's Temple, and they found some defectors who were eager to expose Jones as a fraud. He had sufficient influence to prevent publication of damaging disclosures in the *San Francisco Chronicle*, but a dogged reporter there took his findings to *New West* magazine, which published it despite opposition from politicians and from the American Civil

Liberties Union. Once he knew that a devastating exposé could not be averted, Jones decided to move his sect to Guyana, where he had leased 27,000 acres of land. True to his manner, he warned his people that cruel persecution would befall them, if they remained in the United States, and shortly before the scheduled publication of the dreaded article, Jones and several hundred of his followers left for Guyana. When the *New West* article appeared, it described Jim Jones as a sadistic dictator, a sexual predator, and a manipulator who beguiled people to give him all their worldly goods. He had accumulated assets of about $10,000,000.

The colony in Guyana became a graveyard for Jones and almost all of those who settled there. The paradise he promised was actually a place of unrelieved misery, an inhospitable, insect-infested jungle. Rather than building a habitable community, Jones harangued his people to prepare for enemy attacks, including some from the army of Guyana. The hysteria led him to urge mass suicide through drinking poison, and about nine hundred people died that way. Jones appears to have shot himself. Many children were among the dead.

Survivors of this horror reported that "Jonestown" was a communist society under brutal authority where residents toiled almost as slaves while subsisting on rice. Dissenters were beaten and subjected to various tortures.[39] Stephan Jones, Jim's only biological child, evaded his father's demand for suicide and soon corroborated the horrifying reports of other observers.[40]

The strange career of Jim Jones and the carnage in which it ended comprise one of the greatest tragedies of the twentieth century, a calamity that would not have occurred had not ostensibly Christian people pursued extra-biblical revelation. The magnitude of the catastrophe becomes even more impressive when one realizes that Jonestown was not a singular phenomenon, as the story of the Branch Davidians illustrates.

David Koresh

Born Vernon Howell in 1959, this native of Houston, TX grew up in Dallas as an illegitimate child whose mother reared him in the Seventh Day Adventist Church. In school he had difficulty with his studies and performed poorly until the ninth grade, when he terminated his formal education. From childhood Howell showed much interest in religion and was an avid reader of the Bible. At age eighteen he moved to Tyler, TX, where he joined the local Seventh Day Adventist Church. At some point he became alienated from church leaders who disapproved of his long hair and casual attire at services. Howell responded by leaving that church and joining the renegade sect of the Branch Davidians near Waco.

The Branch Davidians developed as a schism from the Adventists for which Victor Houteff, an excommunicated member of that church, was responsible. In 1929 he founded the Shepherd's Rod Seventh Day Adventist Church, which changed its name to the Davidian Seventh Day Adventist Association in 1942. Houteff claimed to be the latter-day David, of whom the biblical King David was a figure. Houteff's wife Florence assumed leadership of the sect when he died, but when her prediction that Christ would initiate judgment on the world in 1959 failed to occur, her following soon dwindled. One group, however, remained at the compound named Mt. Carmel, and Benjamin Roden, its leader, changed the name to the Branch Davidians. When Roden died, his widow Lois led the movement. She was in charge when Vernon Howell arrived at Mt. Carmel in 1981, soon after the Seventh Day Adventists had excommunicated him. Lois Roden was then sixty-seven years old and Howell twenty-three, but they soon became lovers. By 1988 Vernon Howell wrested control of the cult from George Roden, son of Lois, who died in 1986. The struggle to oust George Roden became vicious and included a gunfight. Howell claimed to be a prophet God had chosen to restore the human race and divine rule over the world. In 1990 this claim led Howell to change his name to David Koresh. The royal name David signified his right to rule over God's people, and, ultimately, over the world. Koresh is the Hebrew name for Cyrus, the Persian king who permitted the Old Testament Hebrews to return from exile to Palestine and to rebuild their temple in Jerusalem.

Sometimes Koresh claimed to be a prophet, at other times Christ himself. He enlisted disciples across the United States and from the United Kingdom, Canada, and as far away as Australia. During 1992 he and his supporters erected a fortress at Mt. Carmel to protect themselves against enemy attacks he said were inevitable. Meanwhile Koresh pursued his interest in rock music and played guitar with several bands from which he recruited followers.

About the time he secured control over the Davidians, Koresh married a fourteen-year-old girl. Thereafter he claimed dozens of "wives," some of them already married to men in the sect. He eventually insisted that all males at Mt. Carmel live without sex, while he would have access to any females he desired. He claimed that divine revelation had authorized him to have one hundred forty wives and to engage in sex with any women he desired, and he alone, as the prophet, had the right to sire children.

An ex-Davidian Elizabeth Barabya said that Koresh claimed

to be a "sinful Jesus" so that, when he stood in judgment of sinners on Judgment Day, he would have experience of all sin and degradation.[41] The prophet of Mt. Carmel liked to cite Psalm 45:7, "your God has anointed you with the oil of gladness," and he held that the "oil" means vaginal fluid to anoint the penis of the prophet. Beyond this absurd use of the Bible, Koresh asserted further that a special revelation had informed him that there are four persons in the Godhead – Father, Mother, Son, and Daughter. The Holy Spirit is the Mother and her daughter would be Koresh's spouse in eternity.[42]

David Koresh never tired of predicting the end of the world was imminent and the biblical battle of Armageddon would soon begin – in Texas! To prepare for the end of all things, he led his people in accumulating weapons. Law enforcement authorities reported that the cult had collected about 8,000 pounds of ammunition. On one occasion a shipment came open while in transit to Mt. Carmel, and it contained hand grenades. The funds to obtain such arms came from donations of the members. Some of them had jobs outside the compound and then gave their earnings to Koresh. Retired members contributed their pensions and Social Security checks.[43]

Like the debacle in Jonestown, the situation at Mt. Carmel became a tragedy. Federal agents, on orders from Attorney General Janet Reno, stormed the compound and encountered stiff resistance. Four officers of the Bureau of Alcohol, Tobacco, and Fire Arms were killed and fifteen wounded. The approximately one hundred people still inside included seventeen children, some of them Koresh's own offspring. With stocks of food, weapons, and power generators, the cult was prepared for a siege, which ended in a holocaust. A composite of federal, state, and local officers launched a final attack after days of fruitless negotiations. Fire erupted during the assault, the cause of which remains a subject of debate to this day. Only a few cult members escaped, and Koresh was among those who perished.

The increasingly secular-materialist worldview of most people in Western Civilization usually leads them to appraise cult leaders such as David Koresh as unscrupulous manipulators bent upon exploiting naïve people for their own pleasure and financial gain. There is abundant evidence to support that view, but, in the case of Koresh, it is a mistake to consider it as the entire explanation. There is, on the contrary, good reason to conclude that both the Branch Davidians and their strange leader sincerely believed his teachings, because a clear and consistent, albeit erroneous, system for interpreting the Bible undergirded the doctrines of the sect.

Koresh's experience as a Seventh Day Adventist disposed him to find in the Bible, especially in the book of the Revelation, predictions about specific developments in modern times. Although the Adventist Church denounced the Waco cult, the hermeneutic of that denomination provided the basis for Koresh's worldview. Ellen G. White (1827-1915), one of the founders of Seventh Day Adventism, claimed to receive direct revelations, which her church regards as inspired counsels from the Lord.[44] Mainstream Seventh Day Adventists have never gone to the extremes which occurred at Mt. Carmel, but their doctrine of continuing special revelation provided a precedent for Koresh to claim prophetic inspirations. He could therefore organize and direct his movement on the basis of what he perceived to be divine instructions. However outlandish his ideas were, to people who accepted him as a prophet, he spoke with the authority of God. Perhaps he, like other cult leaders, lusted for control over other people, but that does not mean he was insincere in his pronouncements. It is not unusual for leaders of ability to convince themselves as well as others that their own ambitions and the will of God are identical.[45]

Despite the calamity at Mt. Carmel, some members of the cult continued to espouse its doctrines. There were efforts to reorganize the movement, and a few resolute Davidians stayed at the desolate property near Waco. A woman whose four sons perished in the fire said she expected David Koresh to return from the dead. Others, such as Amo Bishop Roden, widow of George Roden, said they wanted to purge the sect of Koresh's teachings and restore the original character of the movement. A couple from Mississippi joined her because, they believed, God had told them to do so.[46] Had they not subscribed to extra-biblical revelation by accepting the prophetic gifts of David Koresh, eighty-five people who died in the flames might still be alive. This modern expression of Montanist doctrine shows clearly that false teaching can be deadly to the body as well as the soul.

Marshall Applewhite

Another mystical movement which, by reliance upon extra-biblical revelation, ended in tragedy was Heaven's Gate, a cult which appeared in 1972. It was the creation of Marshall Applewhite (1932-97) and Bonnie Lu Nettles (1928-85), both of whom said they were incarnations of extra-terrestrial beings predicted in the book of Revelation 11:3 as "two witnesses" who would "prophesy 1,260 days" in preparation for the advent of the Kingdom of Heaven. Applewhite was the son of a Presbyterian minister. He met Nettles while in hospital due to a heart ailment. She was a nurse there. After some near-death experience, he became involved with her in astrology and belief in reincarnation. Both Applewhite and Nettles professed to have the gift of prophecy, and they combined elements of Christianity with astrology and a type of mysticism known as New Age philosophy. In 1975, while spreading their ideas in Oregon, they convinced about twenty people from the village of Waldport to follow them to Colorado to meet a spaceship to take them to the "next level," by which they meant heaven.

When the promise of celestial transport failed, the small sect lost credibility and disappeared from public view. By 1994, however, by which time Nettles was dead, Applewhite was again attracting attention by predicting the imminent end of the world, as he traveled across America. People who embraced his ideas came from a broad spectrum of society, and most of them had already been involved with New Age practices. By that time Applewhite was calling his group Total Overcomers, and he purchased a full-page spread in *USA Today* to entice recruits. Those joining him then received instruction in how to prepare for their exit from the world by means of a spacecraft that would take them to the "next level." To finance their programs cult members used their computer skills to compose websites for businesses. Computers were useful in spreading the message of the cult through its own Heaven's Gate website too.

Astrology was a major emphasis of the movement, and belief in UFOs was especially prominent. Applewhite contended that he and Nettles had been brought to earth by UFOs, and he said that the Hale-Bopp Comet housed a spaceship in its tail and it was coming to take him and his followers to heaven.[47] In March 1997, when the comet came closest to earth, and the moon was full, and Christians were observing the end of Holy Week, Applewhite directed his people to discard their "vehicles", that is, their bodies, by group suicide, so their spirits could rise to their celestial home. In the manner of ancient gnostics, the members of Heaven's Gate held to a radical dichotomy of flesh and spirit that reduced the body to the status of a "container" for the soul. Thirty-nine people took poison and perished together, but because of their denigration of the body, they would not have agreed they had actually committed suicide. They, on the contrary, were rising to the "next level."

Some of the most important information about Heaven's Gate comes from former cult members, but unfortunately, their accounts do not always agree. Richard Ford, a computer operator, joined the movement in 1994 and changed his name to Rio Di Angelo (River of Angels). He continued to believe in some of Applewhite's concepts even after he found the decaying corpses of cult members in a suburb of San Diego. He said he hopes to join his departed comrades, but not through suicide. Di Angelo told the story of Heaven's Gate to Mark Miller, who published it in *Newsweek*.[48]

According to Di Angelo, Marshall Applewhite was a persuasive leader able to exert full control over his followers. He forbad alcohol, tobacco, and sex so people could obtain "control of the vehicle" (the body). When some members found the prohibition of sex frustrating, they submitted to castration, as Applewhite himself had done. The prophet said he often conversed with Nettles, who gave him instructions to convey to the membership. Like Jim Jones and David Koresh, Marshall Applewhite feared the government, and in 1995 the sect constructed a fortress of cement and old tires in New Mexico, where the members armed themselves for defense. Nettles, however, intervened, telling Applewhite that a confrontation with civil authorities was not to occur, and that there was no repetition of Waco.

Perhaps the most amazing thing about Heaven's Gate is that the leader was able to convince his followers to renounce the basic human instincts for physical gratification and even survival.[49] When the time came to discard their "containers," cultists did so without compulsion because they believed implicitly in their leader. As one interpreter observed:

> Marshall Applewhite is the herald of a new kind of cult and a new kind of religious fervor — a transcendental zeal that radically despises the world, the body, and the human condition. In that context, Heaven's Gate represents the (literally) terminal form of ancient gnostic behavior.[50]

Most of the people who perished in response to Applewhite's appeal had earlier subscribed to some version of New Age philosophy which stressed astrology, reincarnation, and UFOs, all anti-biblical concepts. Their adherence to the New Age worldview disposed them to seek highly individualistic experiences of truth. One, in fact, claimed that her experience with God had taken place during a time when she was using the drug LSD.[51] Once humans conclude that truth is subjective and relative, a matter of individual preference, there is no logical reason to stop them from joining any cult, however weird it may seem to others.[52]

The, generally supportive, view of Heaven's Gate that Rio Di Angelo expressed in *Newsweek* contrasts sharply with the perspective of Stephen Hill, an ex-cult member, whose wife died along with Applewhite and others, when he could not convince her to leave the cult. Hill portrayed Applewhite as a despotic manipulator who convinced his wife Yvonne McCurdy-Hill to give him the $14,000 she had saved for retirement. Hill contended that the strictly regimented life of the cultists required almost slavish obedience to the leader's prescriptions, which extended to such details as eating and bathing, and to censorship of films, television, and books. The Hills had separated from their four children when they chose the isolation of life with Heaven's Gate. It is noteworthy that Stephen related that Applewhite lived, materially, above his followers. Hill's testimony corroborates the report that Applewhite at one time planned a violent confrontation with law enforcement officials until Bonnie Lu Nettles, speaking from the "next level," told him to abandon that idea. The control the prophet exerted over his followers was, in Stephen Hill's judgment, more dangerous even then a military engagement with the police might have been.[53]

Marshall Applewhite's son Mark, the principal of a Christian school in Corpus Christi, has disavowed his father's beliefs and grieves over the deadly consequences they produced. The elder Applewhite abandoned his family when Mark was only five. Mark now is happy to have God as his real Father, and he prays for people whose gullibility leads them into cults such as Heaven's Gate.[54]

As was true of the People's Temple and the Branch Davidians, the devotees of Heaven's Gate might be alive today, had they not accepted the claims of a self-appointed prophet who said he received special revelation apart from Scripture. All such cults illustrate graphically the biblical precept "the wages of sin is death" (Rom. 6:23). False doctrine is sin, and people who accept it thereby earn the appropriate wages of their offenses against God and his inscripturated Word. The modern versions of Montanism continue to demonstrate the destructive effects of false doctrine.

Evangelical Claims to the Leading of the Lord

Christians should not be surprised by the popularity of belief in extra-biblical revelation among pseudo-Christian cults, but the influence of that presumption among evangelicals is now common and pronounced. This, as the book has already shown, is a conspicuous feature in the teaching of Oral Roberts and Pat Robertson, both of whom are charismatic believers who speak in tongues. Although most evangelicals do not speak in tongues, many of them profess to be in immediate contact with God, whom, they assert emphatically, gives them specific directions in addition to the moral precepts of the Bible. For many such people there is no doubt that Scripture is the Word of God, the inspiration of which they maintain vigorously. Their error lies in a lack of confidence in the *sufficiency* of Scripture as a guide for all of life. It is, for example, not unusual for evangelicals to explain the movement of their membership from one congregation to another as the consequence of the Lord's leading. Pastors sometimes relate that they entered the ministry in response to a divine call in the nature of a vision or an audible voice. At times many Christians make crucial moral decisions, for example, whom to marry, on the basis of an emotional experience they choose to regard as the leading of the Lord. Some of the most popular books by evangelical authors purport to show how believers may discern God's will for all major choices they must make. Living in the *center of God's will* has achieved the status of a pious platitude, a perceived mark of spirituality.

Evangelical authors addressing the matter of divine guidance almost always begin with a clear declaration of confidence in Scripture, while stating categorically that extra-biblical guidance must never contradict God's written Word. Since, however, there are many personal matters which require individuals to choose among alternatives, and Scripture does not address them specifically, there must be other ways of discerning the Lord's will in such matters.[55] Even scholars of the Reformed persuasion have, at times, claimed to receive such personal revelations. Abraham Kuyper (1837-1920), renowned Dutch theologian and statesman, when considering whether to seek a seat in parliament, told a friend, "I have never taken weighty decisions of this kind without receiving a sign from the Lord... I would usually receive such a sign only at the acme of my spiritual strain."[56] A more recent example is the late Francis Schaeffer (1912-84), a Presbyterian minister and distinguished apologist for Christianity and author of many fine books. In 1957 Pastor and Mrs Schaeffer returned from a term of service in Europe in need of a place to live. He prayed for God's provision, while he walked on the balcony of their house in Switzerland. Schaeffer later related that an audible revelation directed him to ask his uncle to open his home. When the uncle did so readily, the Schaeffers concluded that the voice was that of God leading them. One another occasion Francis heard a heavenly voice assure him of forgiveness for his sins.[57] Since Dr Schaeffer was a vigorous champion of orthodox Christianity, it is evident that he did not perceive the tension between the sole authority of Scripture, which he vowed to uphold, and his claim to receive direct communications from God.

Some authors who address the matter of guidance in the Christian life are frank in admitting they do not regard the Bible as sufficient. This is evident in the book *Knowing God's Will and Doing It* by J. Grant Howard, Jr., who earned the degree of Doctor of Theology at Dallas Theological Seminary. He wrote:

> *Is the Bible the only revelation of the will of God for the believer? No, God uses other means to communicate and confirm his will to us, . . .*

> but the Word of God is the primary and sufficient revelation of the will
> of God to the believer. . . . Other factors, such as circumstances, counsel,
> feelings, desires, etc. are involved in discovering and doing God's will,
> but these are secondary and supplementary to the Word.[58]

While appraising extra-biblical means for discerning God's will, Grant included a sense of internal compulsion — "those inner inclinations to do or not to do can be guidelines to God's will." Moreover, he asserted, "how we feel about some action is also an important factor in deciding if it is God's will for us."[59] Grant concluded, "a sense of peace and contentment about a decision is evidence that is what God wants a believer to do."[60] In light of his endorsement of extra-biblical means, it seems odd that Dr Grant Howard, as indicated above, affirmed that the Bible is the *sufficient* revelation of God's will. It what way could it be sufficient, if Christians must pursue other avenues to ascertain God's pleasure? Grant seems to have been unaware of the contradiction in his statements.

Evangelical writers dealing with the subject of divine guidance are most often loyal adherents to the cardinal principles of historic Christianity, so it would be unjust to classify them as Montanist heretics. While it is never their intention to denigrate Scripture, they nevertheless commit the same error that was the basis of Montanism — belief in extra-biblical special revelation, which implies a denial of *sola scriptura*, whatever the intention of those who resort to it.

Perhaps evangelical authors would be more cautious about affirming belief in individual guidance, if they remembered that the pseudo-Christian cults claim some source of revelation apart from or in addition to Holy Scripture. This includes not only recent suicide-sects but older, non-violent ones, such as the Mormons and the Christian Scientists, both of which are heretical.

The Mormons

The religious movement known as Mormonism is officially the Church of Jesus Christ of Latter Day Saints. Its fundamental tenet is belief in continuing special revelation through the gift of prophecy. The Latter Day Saints owe their origin to Joseph Smith (1805-44). A son of a mystical mother, Smith spent his childhood first in Vermont, then in Palmyra, NY, which lay in a region that witnessed a great religious enthusiasm that gave rise to several movements. Smith, still a teenager, was perplexed by the fierce rivalry among churches professing to be Christian, and his mystical inclinations led him to question Protestant teachings and to seek truth in his own way. In 1820 he withdrew into some woods to pray, and he claimed that while he was there, God the Father and Jesus Christ appeared to him in human form. They informed him that all contemporary churches were false. When Smith related this experience to others, he encountered strong criticism and eventually some persecution. For the next three years there were no further revelations.

Then in September 1823, according to Smith's account, an angel named Moroni told him that God chose him as a prophet and that he would find a book inscribed on plates and two stones attached to a breastplate. The stones were the *Urim and Thummim*, of the Old Testament, which Aaron wore when he appeared before Jehovah, whose will he could sometimes discern by means of them (Ex. 28:30; Num. 27:21). The stones, said Moroni, would enable Smith to translate the text on the golden plates. Smith went to a hillside, as the angel directed, and he found a stone box containing the sacred plates. Moroni told him to leave the box there and to visit the site annually for the next four years. On each visit Smith would receive additional instructions about his work as a prophet. When the translation was finished, the *Book of Mormon* became available, and it now holds the status of holy scripture for the Latter Day Saints.[61]

Mormons, as they are known, contend that God chose Joseph Smith to initiate a restoration of genuine Christianity, and they see his work is fulfillment of the Apostle Peter's statement about the ascended Christ, whom "the heaven must receive until the *restitution* of all things" (Acts 3:21).[62] According to Mormon teaching, the restoration of prophecy, miracles, and charismatic endowments began with God's revelation to Smith, and the Church of Jesus Christ of Latter Day Saints is the divinely appointed means to reconstitute the biblical priesthood.

Mormons are frank to indicate that they do not subscribe to the final authority of the Bible. Their *Articles of Faith* document the teachings of their church by citing the *Book of Mormon*, *Doctrine and Covenants*, and *Pearl of Great Price*, to all of which they attribute divine inspiration in the same way that God inspired the writers of the Bible. Mormons do not deny the inspiration of Scripture, but they categorically reject its sufficiency.[63]

Since they maintain that their other inspired writings explain the Bible correctly, the Latter Day Saints believe that they are at liberty to espouse doctrines contrary to the teachings of historic Christianity. They hold, for example, that God is a material being,[64] "the Father and the Son each has a body of flesh and bones as tangible as man's."[65] Mormon doctrine asserts salvation by works.[66] It affirms the atonement of Christ "is made applicable to individual sin in the measure of obedience to the laws of righteousness."[67] In the observance of the Lord's Supper, the Church of Latter Day Saints substitutes water for wine, even though its official publication acknowledges that Jesus used wine when he instituted the sacrament.[68] In true charismatic form, the *Articles of Faith* declare "we believe in the gift of tongues, prophecy, revelation, visions, healing, interpretation of tongues, etc."[69] Contrary to orthodox Christian belief, Mormons contend that salvation is possible for people who die unbelieving, because "repentance may be obtained, under certain conditions, beyond the veil of mortality."[70]

Although the Mormons have not recently been involved in scandals comparable to the People's Temple, the Branch Davidians, or Heaven's Gate, their theology is contrary to biblical teaching, and it justifies regarding their church as a pseudo-Christian cult. The bizarre features of Mormon doctrine would not have developed had not Joseph Smith and others rejected the finality of Scripture as God's only special revelation. The Montanist premise of extra-biblical revelation led the Latter Day Saints into error.

The Christian Scientists

The last of the pseudo-Christian cults to be considered in connection with its view of the authority of Scripture is Christian Science. The teachings of the Church of Christ, Scientist, in some ways are the exact opposite of Mormon doctrine, but both sects, and others already cited, have constructed their systems of belief on extra-biblical foundations.

The founder of Christian Science was Mary Baker Eddy (1821-1910). A native of New Hampshire, she was educated there at a private academy and by personal tutors. She joined a Congregational Church in 1838. As a child she experienced much sickness and was at times subject to hysteria. According to her own account, in 1866 she recovered from intense neck and back pain through miraculous means. This followed a time of study with Phineas P. Quimby, a poorly educated practitioner of homeopathy, who claimed to have found how to exert mental control as a means of healing. He said he had discovered the healing method of Christ: he called his concept the "Science of Christ."

After obtaining relief from pain, Mary Baker (who became Mrs Eddy in 1877) began instructing others in the concept she called Christian Science. In 1875 she published the book *Science and Health*, and to that she added *Key to the Scriptures* in 1883. These works, now bound in one volume, are the authoritative texts of the movement. The Church of Christian Science came into being formally in 1879, with twenty-seven charter members. The Massachusetts Metaphysical College, an institute to train Christian Science healers, began in Boston in 1881. That city is the site of the Mother Church and the Christian Science Publication society. Mrs Eddy founded the *Christian Science Journal* in 1883, and the newspaper the *Christian Science Monitor* in 1908.

At the root of Christian Science teaching is belief in a type of philosophical idealism which contradicts almost every tenet of historic Christianity. Mrs Eddy claimed that she wrote *Science and Health* as God had dictated it to her. Though the book abounds with references to Scripture, it actually supersedes the Bible and is itself the final authority for the church. When Christian Scientists meet for worship, there are no sermons which expound the Scripture. Instead official Readers recite selections from both the Bible and the writing of Mary Baker Eddy without commentary, because her teachings are the last words, the entire truth that never needs exposition.

The fundamental doctrine of Christian Science is the idea that reality is spiritual, and material is a harmful illusion. God is pure spirit, the All in All. God is pure goodness, so all is good. Evil does not exist, and thinking that it does produces harm in the form of suffering. Mind or Spirit alone is real. In the words of Mrs Eddy, "if Mind is within and without all things, then all is mind; and this definition is scientific."[71] Although Eddy scorned pantheism, her concept of God remains vague. She called him the "infinite Principle." He is the "Father Mind . . . not the father of matter,"[72] and God is not a Trinity. She dismissed Trinitarian teaching as polytheism.[73] In the judgment of Mary Baker Eddy, false belief about God and erroneous ideas about man are inseparable, so

> Mortals must change their ideas in order to improve their models. A sick body is evolved from sick thoughts. Sickness, disease, and death proceed from fear. Sensualism evolves bad physical and moral conditions.[74]

The heavy emphasis upon health in Christian Science is evident in its teaching about how to maintain it. True to her worldview, Eddy pontificated, "if one turns away from the body with such absorbed interest as to forget it, the body experiences no pain." Beyond that, "detach sense from the body, or matter, . . . and you may learn the meaning of God, or good, and the nature of the immutable and immortal."[75]

Christian Science's denigration of material creation is entirely incompatible with biblical teaching. It necessitates denial of Christ's incarnation and all that it entails. The Jesus of Christian Science is not the Savior portrayed in the Bible, which affirms clearly that God, who is pure spirit, created the material world, and when he did so, pronounced his handiwork good. In fact, he took pleasure in admiring what he produced (Gen. 1:31). Rather than deploring matter as inherently evil, God took credit for creating it, and he dignified his creation by entering the world of time and matter in the person of Jesus Christ as the "Word became flesh" (John 1:14). Contrary to Mrs Eddy, who contended that evil is not real, God sent his Son into the real world to deal with the real problem of human sin. Christ did not call people to "repent of sin and forsake the unreal," as Eddy maintained. He summoned them to repent for actual sin they commit in the world of flesh and blood. Mary Baker Eddy, however, postulated a radical disjunction between the eternal Christ and the corporeal Jesus. She wrote:

> The invisible Christ was imperceptible to the so-called personal senses, whereas Jesus appeared as a bodily existence. The dual personality of the unseen and the seen, the spiritual and the material, the eternal and the corporeal Jesus manifest in the flesh, continued until the Master's ascension, when the human, material concept, or Jesus, disappeared, while the spiritual self, or Christ, continues to exist in the eternal order of divine Science, taking away the sins of the world, as Christ has always done, even before the human Jesus was incarnate to mortal eyes.[77]

One needs to read only a few pages of *Science and Health* to see how it contradicts plain statements of Scripture. In place of the God-Man of orthodox Christianity, Eddy depicted "Christ, as the true spiritual idea, . . . the ideal of God now and forever, here and everywhere."[78] By categorically denying the essential, eternal deity of Jesus Christ, and by exalting the writings of its founder over the Word of God, Christian Science demonstrates it is a cult, a competitor for real Christianity. Despite Mrs Eddy's claim, "Christian Science is unerring and Divine,"[79] it is a false religion which, like Montanism, has rejected *sola scriptura* and has presumed to speak with an unwarranted prophetic authority. Its teaching is far more radical than that of its ancient prototype, and it is neither *Christian* nor *Scientific*.

The persistence of belief in extra-biblical special revelation across many centuries reflects the expectation that God should demonstrate his power in miraculous ways to verify his claims. Jesus encountered the same demand from scribes and Pharisees. They said, "Teacher, we want to see a sign from you." The Lord answered with a stinging rebuke:

> *An evil and adulterous generation seeks after a sign, and no sign will be given to it, except the sign of the prophet Jonah. For as Jonah was three days and three nights in the belly of the great fish, so will the Son of Man be in the heart of the earth (Matt. 12:39-40).*

When Jesus rose from the dead, and his disciples proclaimed that the sign of Jonah had occurred, most people remained unbelieving. As Paul indicated many years later, "the Jews request a sign, and the Greeks seek after wisdom, but we preach Christ crucified, to the Jews a stumbling block and to the Greeks foolishness" (I Cor. 1:22-23). Christ and his inspired apostles pointed people to the Word of God as the final authority. Even when miracles did occur in the New Testament era, they were not responses to anyone's demand. The authors of the New Testament proclaimed Christ as the capstone of special revelation. He is the supreme miracle, the perfect wisdom of God. His Word, now in written form, is all-sufficient, and no additional revelations will occur until his glorious return. Those who deny this are Montanists-charismatics, even though they may not be aware of it. The finality of Christ and the entire sufficiency of Scripture is the subject of the last chapter in this book.

Notes

[1] Eusebius of Caesarea, *Ecclesiastical History*, tr. Christian Frederick Cruse (Grand Rapids: Guardian Press , 1955), vol. v, 16.

[2] Several contemporaries of Montanus who were in a position to know attested that he made these claims. See *Encyclopedia of Religion and Ethics*, s. v. "Montanism," by H. J. Lawlor.

[3] Eusebius, *Ecclesiastical History*, V, 16.

[4] Hippolytus, *Refutation of all Heresy*, VIII, p. 12 in *Documents Illustrative of the History of the Church*, ed. B. J. Kidd (London: SPCK, 1920), vol. I, p. 169-70.

[5] W. M. Calder, "Philadelphia and Montanism," *Bulletin of the John Rylands Library*, 7 (1923), 327. Cf. William Ramsay, *The Church in the Roman Empire Before AD 170*, 5th ed. (Grand Rapids: Baker Book House, 1954), 437n. Ramsay disputed this view.

[6] A fine biographical sketch of Tertullian appears in *New Catholic Encyclopedia*, s. v. "Tertullian ," by W. Le Saint.

[7] Ramsay, *Church in Roman Empire*, 438-39; Calder, "Philadelphia and Montanism," 328; Bruce, *The Spreading Flame*, 218. There was a sect of unorthodox Jews in Phrygia which could have exerted some influence upon the Montanist idea about continuing revelation. See J. Massingberd, "Was Montanism a Jewish-Christian Heresy?" *Journal of Ecclesiastical History* 17 (1966), p. 145-58.

[8] Tertullian, *De Anima*, C, ix, in *Documents Illustrative of [the] History of the Church*, vol. I, p. 151.

[9] Tertullian, *Adversus Praxean*, pp. 1, 2, 27, 29, in Joseph Cullen Ayer, ed. *A Source Book to Ancient Church History* (New York: Charles Scribner's Sons, 1952), p. 179.

[10] See *Encyclopedia Britannica*, 11th ed. s. v. "Montanism," by H. J. Lawlor.

[11] Timothy Ware, *The Orthodox Church* (Baltimore: Penguin Books, 1963). James Edward McGoldrick, "The Hisorical Need for Creeds and Confessions of Faith," *Reformation and Revival*, 10 (2001), pp. 15-31. This entire issue addresses the importance of confessional Christianity in ways which apply to current trends in evangelical circles.

[12] *The Catechism of the Catholic Church* (New York: Doubleday Publishing Group, 1955), #65.

[13] A useful Roman Catholic study of this matter is that by Laurent Volken, *Visions, Revelations and the Church*, tr. Edward Gallagher (New York: P. J. Kenedy & Sons, 1963).

[14] *Catechism of Catholic Church*, p. 66.

[15] ibid., #67.

[16] ibid., #85.

[17] ibid., #95.

[18] ibid., #97.

[19] ibid., #113.

[20] Edward D. O'Connor, a professor of theology at the University of Notre

Dame, had produced a fine examination of the Roman Catholic charismatic phenomenon in *The Pentecostal Movement in the Catholic Church* (Notre Dame, IN: Ave Maria Press, 1971).

[21] I have witnessed this in person at charismatic services.

[22] An analysis of this appears in Lloyd Billingsley, "Oral Roberts Reports a Seven-Hour Talk with Jesus, Asks for Money," *Christianity Today* (February 18, 1983), p. 29.

[23] Richard N. Ostling, "Raising Eyebrows and the Dead," *Time* (July 13, 1987), p. 55.

[24] Oral Roberts, "Why Miracles Are for Today," *Charisma* (November 1991), pp. 69-74. Negative reactions to Roberts' claims and methods of raising funds have included a damaging attack upon his integrity by former associate Jerry Sholes, whose *Give me That Prime Time Religion* (New York: Hawthorn Books, 1979) is an expose which almost exuded hostility, but he was in a position to know the matters he described, so his book is noteworthy. For a scholarly treatment, see David Edwin Harrell, Jr., *Oral Roberts, An American Life* (Bloomington, IN: Indiana University Press, 1985).

[25] This is an observation from Neil Eskelin, who wrote the laudatory *Pat Robertson, A Biography* (Shreveport, LA: Huntington House, 1987), pp. 56-58.

[26] Ibid., 60-71; for a more scholarly and objective account of Robertson's career, see David Edwin Harrell, Jr., *Pat Robertson, A Personal, Religious, and Political Portrait* (San Francisco: Harper and Row, Publishers, 1987).

[28] Supporters of the rally estimated attendance was 500,000 people. See Harrell, *Pat Robertson*, pp. 176-78.

[29] Quoted by ibid., 180 (emphasis Robertson's).

[30] David Frost, "The Gospel According to Robertson," *US News and World Report* (February 22, 1988), p. 21.

[31] ibid.

[32] Gerald T. Straub, once a staff member at Christian Broadcasting Network, eventually left and became one of Robertson's scathing critics. See his "Salvation for Sale, an Inside View of Pat Robertson's Organization," *Free Inquiry*, 6 (1986), pp. 18-22. A supporter's account of healings appears in Eskelin, *Pat Robertson*, p. 169 ff.

[33] Harrell, *Pat Robertson*, p. 80

[34] This is the judgment of Jeannie Mills, whose book, *Six Years with God* (New York: A. & W. Publishers, 1979), is a graphic account of her experience in the People's Temple, which she wrote after leaving the cult.

[35] ibid., p. 178.

[36] Very informative description of life in People's Temple may be found in "Jim

Jones: Man Who Would Be God," *Christianity Today* (December 25, 1978), 38-40 and Pete Axthelm, Gerald C. Lubenow, Michael Reese, and Linda Walters, "The Emperor Jones," *Newsweek* (December 4, 1978), pp. 54-56, 59-60; James Reston, *Our Father Who Art in Hell* (New York: Times Books, 1981).

[37] Mills, *SixYears*, pp. 180-81.

[38] ibid.

[39] "Jonestown Was a Communist Colony," a report in *Human Events* (December 9, 1978), pp. 2-5, contains explicit details about the sufferings its residents endured. An even more vivid account is that of an American reporter on the site at the time. See Charles A. Krause, *Guyana Massacre, The Eyewitness Account* (New York: Berkeley Publishing Corporation, 1978).

[40] Stephan's story appears in an interview with a reporter. See Cynthia Gorney, "Stephan Jones, Quiet Survivor," *The Washington Post* (November 7, 1983), B1, B8-B9. Cf. "I Escaped People's Temple," *Moody Monthly* (April 1979), pp. 38-41, which is the story of a former cult member as related to Kay Oliver.

[41] Richard Lacayo, "Cult of Death," *Time* (March 15, 1993), p. 38.

[42] See the penetrating analysis of this cult by Hank Hanegraff, "The Branch Davidians: Deadly Delusions," *Christian Research Newsletter* (March-April 1993), p. 5-7.

[43] Lacayo, "Cult of Death," p. 38.

[44] The Seventh Day Adventist teaching about Ellen G. White's role as an inspired messenger is clear in *Seventh Day Adventists Answer Questions on Doctrine* (Washington, DC: Review and Herald Publishing Association, 1957), p. 89-98. For a biographical sketch of the Adventists' founder, see *Great Lives From American History, American Women*, s. v. "Ellen G. White," by James Edward McGoldrick.

[45] A keen analysis of David Koresh which argues that the world in general and the US Government in particular failed to appreciate his genuine religious convictions is the work of James D. Taylor and Eugene V. Gallagher, *Why Waco? Cults and the Battle for Religious Freedom in America* (Berkeley, CA: University of California Press, 1995).

[46] This appeared as an Associated Press dispatch in *Greenville News* (September 7, 1994), 5C.

[47] Stephen J. Hedges, "WWW Mass Suicide," *US News and World Report* (April 7, 1997), pp. 26-30, is a succinct account.

[48] Mark Miller, "Secrets of the Cult," *Newsweek* (April 14, 1997), pp. 29-37.

[49] For a perceptive examination of the cult's worldview, see Peter Jones, "Hell at Heaven's Gate," *Spiritual Counterfeits Project Newsletter*, 21 (Spring 1997), pp. 1-8, 14.

[50] ibid., 3; cf. Robert Balch and David Taylor, "Salvation in a UFO," *Phychology*

Today 10 (October 1976).

[51] Jones, "Hell at Heaven's Gate," p. 7.

[52] The most convenient source of information about New Age ideas is the *New Age Encyclopedia*, compiled by Jerome Clark and Aidan A. Kelly (Detroit: Gale Research, Inc., 1990), which aspires to promote that worldview. A powerful critique is that of John P. Newport, *The New Age Movement and the Biblical Worldview* (Grand Rapids: William B. Eerdmans Publishing Company, 1998). Briefer, more popular analyses are by Douglas R. Groothuis, *Unmasking the New Age* (Downers Grove, IL: InterVarsity Press, 1986), and Herbert J. Pollitt, *The Inter-faith Movement: the New Age Enters the Church* (Edinburgh: The Banner of Truth Trust, 1996).

[53] This interview was with Karl Vick of *The Washington Post*, as it appeared in *Greenville News* (May 3, 1997), 7D.

[54] Douglas Le Blanc, "Seeking Eternal Life Through Death," *Christian Research Journal* (November-December 1997), pp. 6-7, 44.

[55] See M. Blair Smith, *Knowing God's Will* (Downers Grove, IL: InterVarsity Press, 1979), or George Sweeting, *How to Discover the Will of God* (Chicago: Moody Press, 1975).

[56] Quoted by James Edward McGoldrick, *God's Renaissance Man: the Life and Work of Abraham Kuyper* (Darlington, UK: Evangelical Press, 2000), p. 238.

[57] Louis Gifford Parkhurst, Jr., *Fracnis Schaeffer: the Man and His Message* (Wheaton, IL: Tyndale House Publishers, 1985), pp. 74-75.

[58] J. Grant Howard, Jr., *Knowing God's Will and Doing It* (Grand Rapids: Zondervan Publishing House, 1976), pp. 29-30.

[59] ibid., p. 51.

[60] ibid., p. 89; for studies which uphold *sola scriptura* in matters of guidance, see Robert Rayburn, "Finding God's Will," *Covenant*, 13 (April-May 1998), pp. 4-7, 16-17; Sinclair B. Ferguson, *Discovering God's Will* (Edinburgh: The Banner of Truth Trust, 1982); O. Palmer Robertson, *The Final Word* (Edinburgh: The Banner of Truth Trust, 1993); Gary Friesen with J. Robin Maxson, *Decision Making and the Will of God* (Portland, OR: Multnomah Press, 1980); R. B. Kuiper, *God's Will and God's Word* (Philadelphia: Committee on Christian Education, Orthodox Presbyterian Church, n. d.).

[61] James E. Talmage, *A Study of the Articles of Faith* (Salt Lake City, UT: The Church of Jesus Christ of Latter Day Saints, 1952). This is the twenty-eighth printing of the manual of Mormon doctrine, an official statement of all major Mormon beliefs.

[62] ibid., p. 21 (emphasis mine).

[63] ibid., pp. 236 ff; a large portion of this book deals with the doctrine of revelation as it relates to the Bible and other writings believed to be the Word of God.

[64] ibid., pp. 41-48.

[65] ibid., p. 49, quoted from *The Doctrine and Covenants*, 130:22.

[66] ibid., p. 87.

[67] ibid., p. 106.

[68] ibid., p. 175.

[69] ibid., p. 217.

[70] ibid., p. 115. A potent argument against the authenticity of the *Book of Mormon* is the work of Wayne L. Cowdrey, Howard A. Davis, and Donald R. Scales, *Who Really Wrote the Book of Mormon?* (Santa Ana, CA: Vision House Publishers, 1977).

[71] Mary Baker Eddy, *Science and Health with Key to the Scriptures* (Boston: Trustees of the Will of Mary Baker G. Eddy, 1934 rpt. 1875 ed.), p. 287. The major biography of the cult's founder is that by Robert Peel, *Mary Baker Eddy*, 3 vols. (New York: Holt, Rinehart, and Winston, 1977). The author is a Christian Scientist.

[72] Eddy, *Science and Health*, p. 257.

[73] ibid., p. 256.

[74] ibid., p. 260.

[75] ibid., p. 261.

[77] ibid., p. 334.

[78] ibid., p. 361.

[79] ibid., p. 99.

Chapter Three

ANCIENT HERESY: ARIANISM

Greek Rationalism and Christian Doctrine

Almost all of the initial converts to Christianity were ethnic and/or religious Jews, who regarded Jesus as the Messiah and his teachings as the fulfillment of Old Testament predictions. Relatively few of those believers were acquainted with the pagan philosophies then current in the Roman Empire, maintaining instead the Jewish tradition of accepting the truths of their faith on the basis of recognized authority. Subjecting the mysterious features of Christian doctrine to philosophical, rational analysis was not common among them, but when substantial numbers of Gentiles professed the Christian faith, the situation changed, and controversies ensued.

Although Rome ruled the Mediterranean world politically, Greek philosophy dominated the thinking of most Gentile intellectuals, and it gained acceptance among some Jewish scholars as well. The Greeks had a long tradition of speculative inquiry, and their myths abounded with tales of gods who were supermen and half-human and half-divine. The teachings of Plato (427-347 BC) in particular exerted profound influence upon the various schools of thought, each of which adapted his concepts to its own interests. Neo-platonists often denied that God created the material world and human flesh. They postulated a radical dichotomy between flesh and spirit and contended that God, who is pure spirit and goodness, would contaminate himself, were he to contact matter.

Some Greeks argued that matter is eternal, so no creation of the world had occurred. Others held that creation was the work of emanations (aeons) far removed from God. Those Greeks who were monotheists promoted an abstract concept of God as the Supreme Being who had no personal relationship with the material world. To people of this persuasion, a divine incarnation in human form was absurd.

When learned Gentiles acquainted with Greek ideas entered the Church, they soon realized the incongruity between their traditional worldview and fundamental Christian principles which contradicted it. The doctrine of the incarnation in particular caused them much difficulty, so they sought ways to explain it which would satisfy their rationalistic mindset. One approach was to separate the divine Christ from the human Jesus by advocating an adoptionist view comparable to that of the earlier Ebionites.[1] This affirmed the humanity of Jesus but denied his essential, eternal deity. In other words, Jesus was the *Son of God*, but he was not *God the Son*.

Sabellius and Modalism (third century)
Denying the deity of Christ meant rejection of the Trinity

as well, and the most prominent rationalist to do so in the third century was Sabellius, a Libyan, who began to teach the doctrine of modalism about the year 215. This view of the Godhead contends that Father, Son, and Holy Spirit are terms that designate only names of God and do not signify persons. Sabellius taught that all manifestations of God are only expansions of his nature and therefore are only temporary. Jesus Christ then was an earthly manifestation of God's person for a brief period. After completing his work on earth, he no longer existed. He was a mode of God's expression for the redemption of sinners, but that mode ended when Christ's work was finished.

Sabellius illustrated his understanding of God by pointing to the sun. He asserted that the sun as an entity may stand for the Father, while its rays of light signify the Son, and its warming powers the Holy Spirit. As there is one indivisible sun, so God is one and indivisible, although he has expressed himself in three modes. While this view upholds the deity of Christ, it does not do justice to his humanity. Modalism is a rationalistic approach to theology in which philosophic speculation supersedes the authority of divine revelation.

The ancient church rightly rejected Modalism as heresy, and in doing so it affirmed that Christ is the eternal God and an actual human being, distinct in person from the Father and the Spirit, yet one with them in the Godhead. Tertullian (c. 200), a theologian from North Africa, coined the term *Trinity* as a means to clarify the Christian understanding of God and thereby to rebut rationalistic speculations in theology. Earlier authors had clearly affirmed the deity of Christ and the Holy Spirit, but no one had formulated a precise statement to express the character of the Godhead. Tertullian used *Trinitas* (tri-unity), and he referred to the members of the Godhead as persons who shared a common *substantia*. He wrote in Latin, a language with limited usage in the East, where Greek was dominant. As a consequence, this limited his influence in that part of Christendom, which may have contributed to the persistence of theological disputes there. Although church leaders in the West decried Tertullian's affiliation with the Montanists, they appreciated his non-speculative work as a theologian and readily accepted his teaching about the tri-unity of God.

Although the church rejected the teaching of Sabellius, unsound ideas about the person of Christ and the Trinity continued, especially in the East, where scholars engaged in speculative analyses of revealed truth. As a consequence, the church became embroiled in protracted disputes, which threatened the foundations of the faith. Nowhere was this more evident than in the Arian controversy, which compelled the church to state her teaching systematically in creedal form.

Arius (c. 260-336), an elder in the church at Alexandria, being under much Greek influence, taught that the nature of God is indivisible, so there could be no distinction of persons in the Godhead. He held that the Son came into being by an act of the Father, so Christ is a creature, ontologically subordinate to his maker: that is, Christ is by nature inferior to the Father. Arius said, "there was a time when the Son was not." Christ then is not co-eternal with the Father, the only eternal being. Christ is God's first creature, and as the Son, the Father's agent to create the world. Arius believed God had created his Son first, before time, and that he endowed him with some divine properties, but the Son in not inherent deity.

By attributing divine qualities to the Son, Arius portrayed

him as neither fully divine nor fully human. He liked to refer to Jesus as the *Logos*, a Greek term which is prominent in the Gospel of John. Arius understood the statement "the Word [*Logos*] became flesh" (John 1:14) to mean Christ entered history in a God-like appearance because of his *derived* divinity. By denying Christ's eternal and essential deity, Arius, perhaps unintentionally, rejected his finality too. If Jesus were only *like* God, other God-like beings might be forthcoming.[2] Despite his rejection of the Son's eternal deity, Arius urged Christians to worship him because of the divine properties he possessed, and hailed Jesus as the only Redeemer. Arius composed a series of hymns which expressed his Christology and spread his doctrine broadly. His theological position entailed denial of the Holy Spirit's deity as well, and some of his disciples depicted the Spirit as an emanation from Christ.

The Bishop of Alexandria excommunicated Arius about 320; however, the controversy spread quickly across the Eastern Church and aroused the concern of Athanasius (c. 300-73), another Alexandrian theologian. Athanasius was so small in stature that he appeared to be a dwarf, but he was intellectually brilliant, and his devotion to the faith was intense.

At the time Athanasius rose to defend the biblical teaching, supporters of and sympathizers with Arius comprised a majority of church leaders in the East. By then Constantinople was capital of the Roman Empire, and Constantine (r. 306-37) was on the throne, the first Roman ruler to declare himself a Christian. His position in the Arian controversy was crucial to its outcome.

The emperor's understanding of Christian doctrine was meager, and his interest in the Christological debates was at least as much political as religious. Constantine regarded the

Arian question as a serious threat to the unity of his empire, so he decided to intervene. At first he instructed Hosius, his court bishop, to mediate the dispute. When that failed, he summoned all bishops of the church to convene in Nicea, a city near his palace, and prelates from across the Roman Empire attended the first ecumenical council of the church. Of the 400 bishops present, only 6 came from the Western Church, where speculation about the mysteries of the faith aroused relatively little interest.

The Council of Nicea (325) was a factious rather than a homogeneous body, so debates were long and bitter. Some participants accused Arius of idolatry because he considered the Son a creature but urged people to worship him nevertheless. One faction at the council tried to obtain a compromise which would restore peace while allowing some diversity of belief about the relationship of deity to humanity in the person of Christ, but Athanasius insisted on an unequivocal declaration of the Savior's full and perfect deity and humanity, and his convincing eloquence was decisive and effectual.

Athanasius argued that Christ is co-eternal, co-equal, and con-substantial with the Father, and to express this truth he spoke of Christ's *homoousios* with God. This meant that, while Christ is distinct from the Father in person, he is of the same nature, for both the Father and the Son are of one divine essence. The fatherhood of God is an eternal fatherhood, and the sonship of Christ is an eternal sonship. There never was a point where God was not the Father and Christ was not his Son. Athanasius opposed all compromise in the matter and urged the church to issue a statement to which no Arian could subscribe. After much contentious debate, the Council of Nicea adopted the Athanasian position and declared it heresy to deny the eternity of God the Son. Only Arius and two bishops refused to affirm the Creed of Nicea, and the emperor banished them to Illyria, and he ordered the burning of all Arian writings.[3] It appeared that orthodoxy had won a resounding victory, but the Arian opposition was not finished, and rejections of Nicene Christology have punctuated the centuries since the council issued its decision.

Some bishops at Nicea who voted for the creed had little understanding of its importance. Their objective was to restore peace in the church, which to them, was of more consequence than precise declarations of truth. It soon became clear that Arius still had many supporters, and the controversy continued intermittently for sixty years after the council. In 330, while Athanasius was Bishop of Alexandria, the emperor ordered him to reinstate Arius as a presbyter. The bishop refused, and, by defying the emperor, put his life in jeopardy. Constantine retaliated by deposing Athanasius from his bishopric and forcing him into exile. At one point in his contest with the emperor, the bishop went to Constantinople and confronted the ruler while Constantine was riding a horse. Athanasius seized the animal's reins and, while holding the horse in place, said to the emperor, "God will judge between you and me."[4]

Athanasius endured exile several times, but his defense of biblical Christianity prevailed, and he led the way in clarifying the doctrine of the Holy Spirit as well. At a synod of bishops in 362, he persuaded his colleagues to affirm the *homoousia* of the Spirit, which attests to the personality of the Holy Spirit and his eternity and equality with the Father and the Son. A general council of the church meeting at Constantinople in 381 ratified the action the bishops had taken in Alexandria in 362. The biblical-apostolic-catholic doctrine of God now set forth in the Nicene-Constantinopolitan Creed declares:

We believe in one God, the Father Almighty,
Maker of heaven and earth,
of all things visible and invisible.

And in one Lord Jesus Christ, the only-begotten Son of God,
begotten of his Father before all worlds,
God of God, Light of Light,
very God of very God,
begotten, not made, being of one substance with the Father;
by whom all things were made;

who for us and for our salvation
came down from heaven,
and was incarnate by the Holy Spirit of the virgin Mary,
and was made man;
and was crucified also for us under Pontius Pilate;
he suffered and was buried;
and the third day he rose again according to the Scriptures,
and ascended into heaven, and is seated at the right hand of the
    Father;
and he shall come again, with glory, to judge both the living and the
    dead;
whose kingdom shall have no end.

And we believe in the Holy Spirit, the Lord and giver of life,
who proceeds from the Father and the Son;
who with the Father and the Son together is worshiped and glorified;
who spoke by the prophets;
and we believe in one holy catholic and apostolic church;
we acknowledge one baptism for the remission of sins;
and we look for the resurrection of the dead,
and the life of the world to come. Amen.

Throughout the Arian controversy, the Latin Church of the
West had stood with Athanasius, and the creed, of which he
was the principal author, gained almost universal acceptance

across Christendom, and Protestant churches of the Reformation adopted it readily.[5]

The Modern Counterpart: Unitarianism and the Cults

The Persistence of Rationalism

The victory of orthodoxy at Nicea was decisive for the future of the church, but it did not efface rationalistic speculations about the nature of God and the person of Christ. Arianism in a variety of expressions has reappeared often, especially among intellectuals who maintain that belief in God in reasonable, but that the doctrine of the Trinity is absurd. Because they insist on the supremacy of human reason as their authority, such thinkers conclude any belief which appears contrary to reason must be false.

In early modern Europe rationalism became the basis for a worldview popular among savants in various fields of study. Francis Bacon (1561-1626), in his novel *New Atlantis*, predicted reason would one day resolve the mysteries of life and create a paradise on earth. To rationalists such as he, nothing lies beyond the powers of the human mind, so, since Christianity propounds mysteries such as the Incarnation, it cannot be true. Voltaire (1694-1778), foremost of those French thinkers known as *philosophes*, confidently predicted the demise of Christianity within a century because it is an absurd belief. He considered the Bible "a collection of fables, equally outraging good sense, virtue, nature, and the Deity." He regarded Jesus as "a coarse peasant, a fanatic like George Fox," (1624-91), founder of the Society of Friends (Quakers).[6]

For thinkers whose most cherished axiom is the supremacy of reason, the Christian faith is obnoxious. The basic issue between them and the faith they despise is a conflict about authority. Is human reason an autonomous faculty competent to judge all things, or do humans need supernatural revelation in order to understand the world and themselves? Nowhere is this conflict more evident than in disputes about the being of God.

The Trinity and the Two Natures of Christ

A consistent rationalism leads necessarily to rejection of the *ontological* Trinity. Ontology is the study of being. For example, what makes human beings human? Are there particular features of humanity which other beings do not possess? When rationalists seek to understand the being of God, they assume that he must correspond to their conception of what is reasonable. The *philosophes* of early modern history were almost unanimous in affirming belief in a god, because they thought the existence of an orderly universe requires a creator. Some of them regarded the creator as a personal god, while others attributed creation to an impersonal force, but regardless of their disagreement about that, there was broad concurrence about the need for a god.

To affirm a creator-god is, in fact, a reasonable belief, but the Christian doctrine of the Trinity, to many intellectuals, appears to violate the canons of reason. Rationalists seldom doubt the sufficiency and competence of reason. They are highly critical of Scripture, but they do not, as a rule, consider the possibility that reason might be seriously impaired, which is exactly what the Bible teaches. Christian theologians refer to the *noetic* effects of sin, that is, the effects of sin upon human minds. Contrary to the rationalists' assumption, humans are not qualified to judge the claims of God. They have the necessary limitations of creaturehood, and because of their fallen, sinful condition, they do not naturally understand their Creator.[7]

The Apostle Paul was emphatic in asserting the reality of the noetic effects of sin. He wrote, "if our gospel is veiled, it is to those who are perishing, whose *minds* the god of this age has blinded, who do not believe" (2 Cor. 4:3-4 emphesis mine). He warned Christians to avoid the errors of unbelievers who live

> in the futility of their minds, having their understanding darkened, being alienated from the life of God, because of the ignorance that is in them, because of the blindness of their hearts (Eph. 4:17-18 emphasis mine).

Human minds, because of sin, are in an abnormal condition of inability to obtain the proper knowledge of God and the correct understanding of themselves. Therefore they frequently assume they are equipped to judge matters which lie beyond their competence. This tendency is especially pronounced among rationalists who contend the Christian doctrine of God is ridiculous.

Like the ancient Arians, some early modern religious teachers objected to the orthodox Christian doctrine of God because they found it incomprehensible. This attitude became prominent in the era of the Reformation, when rationalists rejected both Catholic and Protestant affirmations of the Trinity and the two natures of Christ. Among the Anabaptists a school of Anti-trinitarian theology emerged in several countries, especially in Italy and Poland.

Socinianism

Since the sixteenth century people who profess belief in God but deny the Trinity have been known as Unitarians, and modern expressions of that view may be traced to the teachings of Lelius Socinus (1525-62) and Faustus Socinus (1539-1604), Italian scholars from a family of learned lawyers. Lelius lost interest in the study of law and turned to theology, dogmatic and mystical. He went to Venice, where a circle of Protestant reformers was meeting, and from there he went to Protestant Switzerland in 1547. While in Geneva he composed *De Resurrectione*, in which he speculated that human souls die with their bodies, and the righteous alone will arise at the return of Christ. This idea and the sympathy he expressed for the condemned Anti-trinitarian Michael Servetus (1509-53) aroused suspicions about his own orthodoxy. Lelius nevertheless was able to convince leading reformers such as John Calvin and Philip Melanchthon to give him letters of recommendation to Protestant leaders in Poland. After a period of travel, he returned to Switzerland, where he settled in Zurich. Despite his doubts about the deity of Christ, Lelius was able to satisfy Heinrich Bullinger (1504-76), the chief Reformed pastor in the city, and there Lelius remained until he died in 1562.

Faustus Socinus, nephew of Lelius, was more influential than his uncle, who convinced him to embrace unconventional ideas about theology. Like Arius of the fourth century, Lelius and Faustus believed that Jesus was a superior human being whom God had endowed with some divine properties. He was the Son of God but not God the Son.

Faustus fled from Italy in 1561 to avoid persecution by Roman Catholic authorities. As a refugee in Zurich he obtained some of his uncle's writings, and reading them emboldened him to become an exponent of Anti-trinitarian theology. Faustus followed Lelius in writing an exposition of the first chapter in the Gospel of John from a heterodox point of view.

Despite his advocacy of heretical views, Faustus was able to gain employment in Italy with Grand Duke Cosimo I, who protected him during the years 1563-75. Soon after Cosimo died, Faustus returned to Switzerland and lived and wrote in Basel. Perhaps his most significant book is *De Jesu Christo Servatore (Jesus Christ the Saver)*, which he finished in 1578, but which was not published until 1594. In that treatise he denied that the death of Christ satisfied the wrath of God against sinners.

In 1579 Faustus moved to Poland, where he married and remained until he died. During that phase of his life, he became the leader of the Polish Brethren, an Anti-trinitarian, Anabaptist body, for which he was the chief apologist. He wrote to refute the doctrines of the Trinity and the Incarnation, and he directed the compilation of the *Racovian Catechism* (1605). This work, translated into several languages, helped to spread the rationalist approach to theology in general, and it influenced readers to reject historic Christianity by denying the essential, eternal deity of Christ. When persecution occurred in Poland, Socinians fled to Hungary, Germany, England, and the Netherlands, where they promoted their Unitarian beliefs.[8]

Unitarianism in America

When Socinian teachings became evident in England, Parliament forbad promulgating them, but they spread despite occasional suppression. By the eighteenth century, some clergymen in the Church of England and some non-conformists as well embraced Socinian-Unitarian theology, and the first Unitarian assembly appeared in 1778. Within the Anglican Church Joseph Priestly (1733-1804), a celebrated scientist, promoted a Unitarian view of God and encouraged the Established Church to tolerate it. The Church of England showed itself receptive to that appeal, even though its *Thirty-Nine Articles of Religion* are unequivocally Trinitarian. Priestly preached Unitarian doctrine while he was pastor at Leeds and Birmingham, but opposition led him to leave for America in 1794. He went to Philadelphia and soon founded two congregations. The one at Northampton, Pennsylvania, was the first in America to assume the name Unitarian. Priestly was confident his religious persuasion would be the wave of the future, that it would sweep across the country and win a huge following.[9]

Although Philadelphia was the birthplace of Unitarianism in America, Boston was the site of its prosperity, and the most distinguished figures of the movement were scholars at Harvard College and Harvard Divinity School. Perhaps the most prominent of the early New England Unitarians was William Ellery Channing (1780-1842), who contended that Unitarianism was a correction of Calvinism, and he maintained the dispute between those faiths was due to conflicting interpretations of Scripture. Channing, pastor at Federal Street Church, Boston, called for a "reasonable" use of the Bible. He expressed this in a sermon entitled *Unitarian Christianity*. Rationalism and moralism, he asserted, are the essential components of religion. Channing portrayed God as a loving Father, a view, he thought, that contradicts Reformed theology. He rejected the deity of Christ and argued that Jesus' mission had been to initiate a moral and spiritual deliverance of humanity by teaching and through his outstanding example. In one sermon Channing urged his hearers to realize the "Divinity within us."[10]

The Unitarians' control of Harvard College assured them great influence throughout New England and beyond. The extent of their leverage became clear when Henry Ware (1764-1845) obtained the Hollis Chair of Divinity in 1805 over the protests of orthodox pastors, who knew that chair bore the name of Thomas Hollis, a Puritan from London, who had endowed it. The inability of those pastors to keep Ware off the faculty is evidence of Puritanism's declining strength, and to combat the trend at Harvard, conservatives founded Andover Theological Seminary in 1808. The liberals responded by creating Harvard Divinity School, which became a stronghold of Unitarian teachings.[11]

Unitarianism, in its formative years, was the work of liberal Congregationalists in Boston and eastern Massachusetts who had forsaken their Puritan heritage and adopted rationalism. All prominent churches of that connection in Boston, except one, became Unitarian eventually, and the polity of Congregationalism made it difficult to keep liberals out of its pulpits. First Congregational Churches embraced Arminian teaching about sin and salvation, and later they accepted Unitarian theology.[12]

Always at the root of Unitarian thinking was firm confidence in the authority of reason. As one of its enthusiastic advocates wrote, "Christianity or the doctrines of revealed religion came to be interpreted as a system of divine *Truth* adapted to reason and common sense."[13] Confidence in the human intellect without regard for the noetic effects of sin took precedence over Scripture, while Unitarians nevertheless insisted they were exponents of genuine Christianity. In 1865, when they formed a National Conference of Unitarian Churches, they adopted a constitution for Christian Churches of the Unitarian Faith.[14]

As Unitarians developed their body of beliefs, they demonstrated clearly their departure from historic

Christianity, not only with regard to the nature of the Godhead but on other doctrines too. Boston intellectuals organized the Anthology Club, out of which came several periodicals and eventually the *Unitarian Review*. Through such publications liberal religion spread its denial of human depravity and asserted its belief in the nobility of human nature. Theodore Parker (1810-60), a Harvard graduate and pastor in Boston (1849-59), was one of the most eloquent champions of Unitarian ideas about God and man. He argued that the permanent values of Christianity are its teachings about morality, which are best expressed in social services to meet humanity's material needs. Parker contended that socialism is the most appropriate means to implement the teachings of Jesus, and he denied emphatically that a loving God would punish anyone eternally.[15]

Although most Unitarians of the nineteenth century considered themselves Christians, it is evident that they abandoned some of the foundational doctrines of the faith. To justify retention of the label *Christian*, some of them re-defined the term. Consider, for example, this statement from Henry Whitney Bellows (1814-82):

> the name Christian does not rest . . . on any theory whatever about the nature or office or person or doctrine of Christ. It rests simply on the fact that we are Christian by habit or inheritance unless we deliberately choose to renounce that name in favor of some other.[16]

In other words, one may rightly assume the identity of a Christian regardless of his or her belief about the person and work of Jesus Christ. In fact, accommodation to the worldview of modern culture is necessary for the survival of Christianity. As Unitarian author Joseph Henry Allen asserted in 1892, "religion may yet be saved whole and unharmed ...

but only by that cordial co-working with the spirit of the time, which is the very thing we mean by a liberal faith."[17]

As Unitarians became progressively elastic in their thinking, a vague theism emerged which satisfied their rationalist worldview and allowed for great diversity of belief among them. Some came to espouse a frank humanism in which the term *god* was only a symbol for human religious aspirations.[18]

Universalism

As the dictum of Theodore Parker about eternal punishment shows, within Unitarian ranks there was great receptivity to the doctrine of universal salvation. Side-by-side with the growth of Unitarian churches, a body of avowed universalists developed as initiated by the work of John Murray (1741-1815), an English immigrant who became a chaplain for the American troops during the War for Independence. Although Murray had a Calvinistic heritage, he became an Arminian due to the influence of Methodist preacher John Wesley. Eventually Murray denied everlasting punishment of lost sinners because he thought Christ had atoned for all sinners, so all people must be saved. In 1774 Murray went to Gloucester, Massachusetts, where he founded a Universalist Church in 1779. In 1793 he moved to Boston, where he remained until his death, and from Boston he traveled to preach in many other places.

Elhanan Winchester (1751-97) was another pioneer Universalist. In 1780 he became pastor of First Baptist Church in Philadelphia, but his belief in universal salvation was not acceptable to his congregation. He therefore soon left that church and took a number of its members with him, and they organized their own church. Winchester was an outspoken exponent of Universalism, and his eloquence attracted many people to his doctrine. In 1790 a Philadelphia Convention of Universalists created the first ecclesiastical organization of that persuasion. A New England Convention of Universalists came into being in 1792. Winchester drafted a statement of principles, which the New England Convention adopted as the *Winchester Profession* in 1803. Like many Unitarians and like John Murray, Winchester's acceptance of anti-Christian teachings was due to the influence of Arminianism. He believed the Arminian doctrine that Christ atoned for the sins of everyone, and from that premise, he concluded that all people will be saved.

The works of John Murray and Elhanan Winchester notwithstanding, the most influential theologian of early American Universalism was Hosea Ballou (1771-1852), who led Universalists to embrace the Unitarian concept of God. Ballou disavowed the Reformed teaching about election to salvation and the particular redemption of the elect alone, but he went further by contending that the death of Christ was not a sacrifice to reconcile the holy God and the sinful humanity. His understanding of this matter appeared in a book entitled *A Treatise on Atonement* (1805). Ballou held that punishment for sin is always corrective. Christ on the cross displayed God's love for sinners, and the influence of Christ's death and his teachings brings people to seek moral rehabilitation. According to his view, sinners who refuse to follow Christ's moral precepts will experience repentance after death, so there will be no eternal punishment. Ballou was a pastor in New Hampshire, Vermont, and Massachusetts, and he ended his career at Boston's Second Universalist Society (church).[19]

Gradually Unitarians and Universalists drew together

and declared common belief in the Fatherhood of God and the brotherhood of man and universal salvation. Both bodies conceived of religion as a means to improve society. A man-centered faith became ever more evident among them, as they focused on earthly problems and almost ignored eternity. True to their Arian-rationalist axioms, they regarded Jesus as a profound teacher and an inspiring example, but they had no place for the biblical God-Man and Savior of sinners. Universalists and Unitarians merged in 1961 by forming the Unitarian Universalist Association. Their common rationalist worldview and mutual hatred for Calvinism with its emphatic God-centeredness brought them together.

Although the Unitarian Universalist Association is a small denomination, its ideas have won disciples in several major Protestant churches which tolerate diversity of belief while continuing to regard themselves as Christian bodies. Arianism in various forms is alive and well, flourishing in modern liberal churches.

Christ and the Cults

Denial of the ontological Trinity and the two natures of Christ, a prominent feature of religious liberalism, is characteristic of pseudo-Christian cults as well. Unitarians dismiss historic Christian doctrine because they regard it as offensive to reason, but the cults, as a rule, do so because they claim the Bible does not teach Trinitarian theology. As chapter two of the present book shows, Christian Science denies Jesus Christ is the God-Man, and so it is to be regarded as a cult.[20] The Mormons, who claim to be Trinitarians, and the Jehovah's Witnesses, who deny the tri-unity of God, illustrate well the continuing influence of Arianism even among people who profess to believe the Bible.

The Mormons

Although Mormon literature contains many references to God as a Trinity, the Latter Day Saints do not affirm the orthodox Christian doctrine of the Godhead. The *Articles of Faith*, the official Mormon manual of teaching, asserts, "we believe in God the eternal Father, and in His Son Jesus Christ, and in the Holy Ghost."[21] While this statement appears Christian as far as it goes, it does not go far enough. Mormons do not believe in God as one being in three eternal persons. They instead regard the Father, the Son, and the Holy Spirit as three separate beings, which is a form of polytheism or at least tri-theism. According to the official teachings of the Latter Day Saints, the term Trinity does not signify the Father, the Son, and the Holy Spirit are all of one substance or divine nature.[22] There is a unity of will and purpose among the divine persons, but they are not one in being. The Mormon description of God states:

> Both the Father and the Son are in form and stature perfect men; each of them possesses a tangible body, infinitely pure and perfect and attended by transcendent glory, nevertheless a body of flesh and bones.
>
> The Holy Ghost . . . is not tabernacled in a body of flesh and bones, but is a personage of spirit, yet we know that the Spirit has manifested himself in the form of a man.[23]

While Mormons do attribute personality to the Father, the Son, and the Holy Spirit, they fail to appreciate the ontological unity of the Godhead. By ascribing materiality to the Father and the Son, while contending that the Holy Spirit has no physical nature, they not only contradict Scripture, they postulate a radical discrepancy within the Godhead. What they mean when they assert the Holy Spirit has "manifested himself in the form of a man" is not clear, and it seems to contradict their own denial of materiality to the Spirit.

Confusion about the Mormon doctrine of God is due in part to evident conflicts between statements in the *Book of Mormon* and some declarations of Joseph Smith, founder of the Latter Day Saints. The *Book of Mormon*, in places, seems to affirm a Trinitarian theology, as for example, "this is the doctrine of Christ, and the only true doctrine of the Father, of the Son, and of the Holy Ghost, which is one God, without end" (2 Nephi 31:21). The same source says about the coming judgment of humans, they "shall be . . . arraigned before . . . Christ the Son, and God the Father, and the Holy Spirit, which is one eternal God" (Alma 11:44). Such statements appear to affirm belief in the ontological Trinity.

In some of Joseph Smith's writings a different theology appears. Mormonism's most revered prophet taught there are many gods. In a sermon Smith delivered in 1844, he proclaimed:

> *I have always declared God to be a distinct personage, Jesus Christ a separate . . . personage from God the Father, and that the Holy Ghost was a distinct personage, . . . and these three constitute three distinct personages and three Gods.*[24]

Smith maintained the Bible teaches a plurality of gods, and he cited I Corinthians 8:5, "there are many gods and many lords," to support his contention. It is evident Smith ignored the context and character of this passage, because the expression he quoted is part of the Apostle Paul's critique of idolatry and pagan veneration of gods that do not exist. The Apostle stated emphatically, "there is no other God but one," and he rejected all others as "so-called gods" (I Cor. 8:4-5).

However the Latter Day Saints may try to harmonize the teachings of their prophet with the *Book of Mormon*, the discrepancy remains. Either Smith taught falsehood, or the sacred book of the Latter Day Saints is in error. In either case the damage to Mormonism's credibility is obvious.

Although the *Book of Mormon* appears to teach monotheism in a Trinitarian manner, other sacred writings of the cult refer to numerous gods. It is evident that Smith's concept of God developed over time from monotheism to polytheism. In the *Doctrine and Covenants* Smith referred to plural deities who comprise a council of gods over which the eternal God presides (121:32), and he promised faithful Mormons they would become gods (132:20), as Abraham, Isaac, and Jacob have already attained deity. The *Doctrine and Covenants*, however, does place such gods in subjection to the Supreme God, who alone is worthy of adoration (20:19). However vague his teaching about God and gods, it is clear Smith extended to his followers the prospect of achieving deity in some sense of that term.

The elasticity with which Mormon writers use the term *God* makes it difficult to understand how they regard the person of Jesus Christ. They maintain strongly that he existed with the Father before his incarnation and that he became man through a miraculous conception in the Virgin Mary's womb. He is therefore the Son of God, but not in the way Christians historically have understood his sonship.

Latter Day Saints hold that all human souls existed in eternity before they received fleshly bodies on earth. Christ was the first of the spirits the Father created in eternity. A passage in the *Pearl of Great Price* asserts that Christ and Satan are both, "from the beginning" (Moses 4:1-2), and J. E. Talmage explained that Christ and Satan then "existed as intelligent individuals, possessing power and opportunity to choose the course they would pursue and the leaders whom they would follow and obey."[25] Despite other affirmations about the deity of Christ in various Mormon sources, this passage and Talmage's explanation demonstrate that the Latter Day Saints do not espouse orthodox Christology. If Christ and Satan were both "from the beginning," were they both eternal? Perhaps so, if God created them in eternity before time began. If that is so, Christ and Satan are creatures nevertheless, since at some point in eternity they came into being. Beyond this deduction, it is appropriate to ask if all human spirits are eternal in the same way as Christ and Satan. This belief conflicts sharply with historic Christian teaching that Christ is eternal and there never was a point when he did not exist, and it denies that humans are temporal creatures whose existence begins at conception in their mother's wombs.

Do Mormons consider Jesus Christ one god among many? Does his deity consist in an exalted status conferred upon him before time? Parley P. Pratt, one of the most influential of Mormon theologians, described Christ in these terms:

> Here, then, we have a sample of an immortal God, a God who is often declared in the scriptures to be like His Father . . . and possessing the same attributes as His Father, in all their fullness; a God not only possessing body and parts, but flesh and bones and sinews, and all attributes, organs, senses, and affections of a perfect man.[26]

Although Christians reject the contention that God is a material being, they concur that Christ is fully and perfectly human as well as divine, but they believe deity is inherently his, since he is not a subordinate god created in time or eternity. Literal immortality belongs to Christ because, as God, he is without beginning and end. Pratt, however, has identified him as "*an* immortal God." Does the indefinite article not indicate one god among others? It appears that Mormon theologians view Christ as distinct from the Father in being as well as in person. He is then a *divine creature*, however strange that term may seem.

Mormons do not agree that Jesus Christ possesses two entire natures, human and divine. They cannot subscribe to this tenet of historic Christianity because they think God and humans have the same nature: "Gods, angels, and men are all of one species, one race, one great family, widely diffused among the planetary system."[27] This at least implies denial of the Creator-creature distinction, which is the fundamental point of reference in Holy Scripture. It should now be clear that Mormon theology and Christology are not Christian, even though the Latter Day Saints use the same language as Christians with reference to God and Christ. In the manner of ancient Arians, Mormons regard Jesus Christ as the Son of God but not God the Son. They portray him as the Father's foremost creature endowed with some divine qualities. As James Talmage expressed their view, to Mormons Jesus was "invested with the powers and rank of Godship."[28] According to this teaching, Christ is neither fully God nor fully man.

The Jehovah's Witnesses

Among competitors with Christianity, the Jehovah's Witnesses are perhaps the most vigorous. The movement originated in the work of Charles Taze Russell (1852-1916), who came from a Presbyterian family in Pittsburgh, Pennsylvania. As a teenager Russell moved to the Congregational Church, but he reacted against the doctrines of election and eternal punishment and soon abandoned Christianity. In 1870, however, due to the influence of the Seventh Day Adventists, he renounced his skepticism and began studying the Bible and teaching his understanding of it to others. The Seventh Day Adventists expected the return of Christ in the flesh, but Russell held that it would be an invisible, spiritual event. Russell and his followers joined with a group from Rochester, New York in 1876, and the merged body established congregations and began publishing religious literature. His joint ventures with N. H. Barbour, leader of the Rochester group, did not last long, due to doctrinal disagreements. In 1879 Russell began publishing *Zion's Watchtower and Herald of Christ's Presence*, and in 1881 he formed Zion's Watchtower Society, which soon became Watchtower Bible and Tract Society, which is still its official name.

The Watchtower Society has distributed millions of items of literature throughout the world, and Russell's own writings have circulated widely. His book *The Divine Plan of the Ages* has been very influential.[29] He claimed to understand the Bible correctly, and he contended that no one could obtain the truth from Scripture without his explanations.[30] Russell did not resort to extra-biblical revelations, but he professed to be the indispensable expositor of Scriptural truth.

Upon the death of Charles Russell in 1916, Joseph Franklin Rutherford (1869-1942) became president of the Watchtower Society, a position he held until his own death. Rutherford, who came from a Baptist family, was a lawyer, and for a short time, a circuit judge in Missouri. He embraced Russell's teachings in 1906 and became legal advisor to the Watchtower Society. As second president of the organization he was an effective leader, but his dynamic style offended some of the members, who seceded and formed separate sects. During World War I Rutherford aroused the ire of the American and Canadian governments by declaring the neutrality of the Watchtower Society. Canada banned distribution of the group's literature, and the United States arrested Rutherford and some other leaders of the cult for sedition. Although a federal court sentenced them to twenty years in prison, an appellate court freed them after less than a year. Rutherford was a prolific author, and his writings eventually superseded those of Russell as standard texts for the Society.

In 1931 the Watchtower Society met in convention at Columbus, Ohio, and there adopted the name Jehovah's Witnesses officially. The basis for this name is a statement in Isaiah 43:10, "you are my witnesses and my servant whom I have chosen." By this time Judge Rutherford had cemented his position as the pre-eminent authority in the Society, and his administration in Brooklyn, New York operated as a "theocratic kingdom" which dispatched its agents around the world.

Both Russell and Rutherford made predictions based upon their computations from biblical data. They always insisted the Bible was their standard, for it is the inerrant Word of God. *Let God Be True*, a manual of doctrine for Jehovah's Witnesses, asserts:

> *knowing that God by his holy spirit inspired the Holy Scriptures, thus making them reliable, we choose to let him do the interpreting.*[31]

The Jehovah's Witnesses affirmation of confidence in Scripture is, of course, commendable. Their manner of using the Bible, however, displays that they assign greater authority to human reason than to God's written Word. Like ancient Arians and modern Unitarians, teachers of the Watchtower Society reject as unreasonable and therefore false the eternal, essential deity of Jesus Christ and the doctrine of the Trinity. They caricature orthodox theology by claiming historic Christianity teaches "there are three gods in one."[32] The actual Christian position is that there is *one God in three persons*. Monotheism is the bedrock of biblical revelation, a position Christians have always maintained. Jehovah's Witnesses claim that Jesus is the Son of God but not God the Son. One of their recent books about Christ states, "he was a very special person because he was created by God before all other things."[33] Christ then is the first and foremost of God's creatures who, "because he carefully imitated his heavenly Father, . . . was the greatest man who ever lived."[34]

If the Watchtower doctrine of Christ is correct, the Christian belief in God's triune being is, obviously, absurd. Publications of the Witnesses assert the doctrine of the Trinity is an unscriptural tenet that arose in the second century and became dogma in 325 at the Council of Nicea. Their handbook of doctrine contends "Satan is the originator of the trinity doctrine."[35]

In order to support their view that Christ is a creature, Jehovah's Witnesses have produced their own translation of the Bible, one which contains renderings almost unique to itself, as, for example, John 1:1-3:

> *Originally the Word was, and the Word was with God, and the Word was a god. This one was originally with God. All things came into existence through him, and apart from him not even one thing came into existence.*[36]

An explanatory note on this text relates that the *Word (Logos)* is "a god" in contrast with "the God." The identity of the Word is not in doubt, for verse 14 of this chapter affirms, "so the Word became flesh and resided among us" (New World Translation). Jehovah's Witnesses understand this *Word* to be Jesus Christ, God's first human creature and his agent for the creation of the universe and of all other human beings.

109

Watchtower authors cite the absence of the definite article before *God* in the Greek text of John 1:1, and their New World Translation has the indefinite article *a god*, and "this proves that two persons are spoken of as being with each other, and not two persons as being one and the same God."[37] Although this interpretation of the *Logos* may seem plausible, a careful examination of the passage does not support it, and specific affirmations of the New Testament about the deity of Christ contradict it.

The omission of the definite article is due to the word order in which God (*Theos*) comes first. In English it would be awkward to say "the God loves me," and in the Greek New Testament the term for God often appears alone, that is without the definite article.

Never does Scripture state or imply there is more than one God. John 1:1 and other biblical passages recognize a distinction of persons within the Godhead while maintaining strict monotheism. The Gospel of John itself fairly abounds with declaration of Christ's essential, eternal deity, as for example, in chapter 14:1-11, which relates that Jesus said, "he who has seen me has seen the Father" (14:9). Jesus, when in controversy with some Jews, offended them by asserting, "before Abraham was I AM," and his critics understood this to be a claim to deity, so they attempted to stone him for making it (8:58-59). After his resurrection Jesus appeared to Thomas, a doubting disciple, who then hailed the Savior as "my Lord and my God." Jesus was pleased with this ascription and pronounced a benediction upon others who do the same (20:24-29). Other New Testament authors too affirmed the Savior's deity. See Philippians 2:5-11, Colossians 2:9, Romans 9:5, Titus 2:13, and Hebrews 1:1-3.[38]

Despite their contention that Scripture is their only authority, teachers of the Watchtower Society approach God's Word with rationalistic axioms, and they fail to let Scripture speak for itself. As an example, consider Isaiah 9:6, which Christians cite as a messianic prophecy which identifies the coming Savior as "mighty God." Although the clarity of this term (Hebrew *el Gibor*) attests to the deity of the Messiah, Jehovah's Witnesses claim it refers to "*a* Mighty God, but not *the* Almighty God, Jehovah."[39] If this conclusion is valid, Jehovah's Witnesses are polytheists, since they regard Christ as a divine person less than Jehovah-God. The Christology of the Watchtower Society is a modern version of the Arian heresy. Like the ancient Arians, this cult teaches that Jesus became the Messiah (Christ) by adoption at his baptism in Jordan River.[40]

Since Jehovah's Witnesses promulgate false teaching about the person of Christ, it should surprise no one that they maintain a deficient view of the Savior's work as well. They do not extend the hope of deification to their faithful members as the Mormons do, but still they portray the doctrine of salvation wrongly. Not only do they denigrate Christ to the status of a creature, they deny the sufficiency of his redeeming sacrifice and his bodily resurrection.

Watchtower publications often refer to Christ's death as a sacrifice which obtained "a redemption accomplished, not by wealth or ability of man, but by a provision of God,"[41] and they affirm Christ as the only Savior, so "forgiveness of sins and salvation to eternal life [are] possible only through Christ."[42] At first glance this appears to be orthodox doctrine, but further investigation will show it is not. The authoritative manual *Let God Be True* declares:

> All who by reason of faith in Jehovah God and in Jesus Christ dedicate themselves to do God's will and then faithfully carry out their dedication will be rewarded with everlasting life (Rom. 6:23).[43]

The concept that eternal life is a *reward* conflicts with the very proof-text cited to support the above assertion. Romans 6:23 states clearly "the gift of God is eternal life in Christ Jesus our Lord." A *gift* is an unearned favor, but Jehovah's Witnesses claim admission to heaven awaits only those people who comprise the 144,000 of Revelation 14:1-5, "who have been purchased [redeemed] from the earth" (New World Translation). These heroes of faith earn the heavenly reward by sacrificing their right to live on a restored earth, which they obtain through the work of Christ. In other words, heaven is only for those who gain it by their own sacrificial merits.[44] It appears the teaching of the Watchtower Society confines the benefits of Jesus' redeeming work for most people to eternal residence on planet earth.

A crucial test of any religion is to ascertain what it espouses regarding the resurrection of Christ, for Scripture proclaims, in the words of the Apostle Paul, "if Christ is not risen, your faith is futile: you are still in your sins" (1 Cor. 15:17). Jehovah's Witnesses deny the bodily resurrection of Christ and contend "he came forth from the grave, not a human creature, but a spirit."[45] The biblical Christ, however, is not a creature but the God-Man who possesses a complete human nature, body and soul. When he appeared to the Apostle Thomas, who had doubted reports of the Lord's resurrection, Jesus displayed his actual body and said to his disciple "reach your finger here, and look at my hands; and reach your hand here and put it into my side." This demonstration of Jesus' bodily actuality convinced Thomas and led him to acclaim Jesus as "my Lord and my God" (John 20:27-28).

Although Jesus appeared in his glorified state, his humanity was genuine, and his resurrection was not a mere spiritual manifestation. He is now in heaven, where he serves his redeemed people as their mediator with the Father. As the Apostle Paul stated, "there is one God and one mediator between God and men, the *man* Christ Jesus' (I Tim. 2:5-6, emphasis mine). Christ is there in his fullness, which includes his perfect humanity.[46]

Throughout the literature of the Watchtower Society there are appeals to human reason to judge the Word of God. When biblical declarations appear to conflict with what Jehovah's Witnesses consider reasonable, their publications offer alternatives to historic Christian beliefs. Doctrines such as the Trinity and the two natures of Christ are unacceptable because they seem to be impossible. Objections of this sort, like those from other pseudo-Christian cults, are not new. They, on the contrary, are but modern versions of ancient Arianism. Together with the Unitarians, the cults, at least in practice, postulate the supremacy of the human mind over the revealed Word of God. In doing so they display the noetic effects of sin, which lead people to employ reason perversely. Humans should realize the limitations of creaturehood, compounded by the effects of sin on their minds, make some revealed truths incomprehensible. This is due in large part to the depraved condition of the mind. Regenerate thinkers submit to the authority of Scripture, where God presents his self-disclosure, and they admit their own ontological and moral limitations readily. They do not presume to have a comprehensive knowledge of their Creator.[47] Subscription to *sola Scriptura* is the hallmark of genuine Christianity which distinguishes it from competing systems of belief. Christians adore and serve the Christ of the Bible, the God-Man who, as the ancient church affirmed in the Creed of Nicea, "for us and for our salvation came down from heaven, and was incarnate by the Holy Spirit of the Virgin Mary." This Christ is the second person of the Godhead, wherein, as the *Westminster Shorter Catechism* declares, the three persons are "one God, the same in substance, equal in power and glory" (question 6).

All historic creeds and confessions affirm belief in the ontological Trinity. All of the cults deny it. Christians admit the Trinity is beyond human ability to understand, but they do not regard Trinitarian theology as unreasonable. With Martin Luther they contend, "it is not Christianity which needs to be made reasonable, but reason that needs to become Christian." Regeneration by the Holy Spirit imparts faith to believe mysteries that human minds cannot fully comprehend.

Rejection of the Trinity and the two natures of Christ is characteristic of the Anti-Christ (2 John 7-11). Arianism and Unitarianism are not versions of Christianity but competing religions. Fallen reason is their authority, and they arrogantly judge God's claims about himself. Arianism, in both its cultic and ecclesiastical expressions, is a rival to genuine Christianity.[48]

Notes

[1] See chapter one.

[2] This is the view of Rousas J. Rushdoony, *The Foundations of Social Order* (Philadelphia: Presbyterian and Reformed Publishing Company, 1972), p. 15.

[3] Interesting analyses of the Arian controversy appear in Robert Payne, *The Holy Fire* (London: Skeffington & Son, 1958) and Hermann Dörries, *Constantine the Great*, (New York: Harper & Row, 1972).

[4] Quoted by Payne, *Holy Fire*, p. 116.

[5] For examination of the creedal posture of Protestantism, see James Edward McGoldrick, "The Historical Necessity for Creeds and Confessions of Faith," Reformation and Revival, 10 (Spring 2001), pp. 15-31.

[6] Quoted by Frederick B. Artz, *The Enlightenment in France* (Kent, OH: Kent State University Press, 1968), 80; Stephen J. Tonsor, "History, a Revolutionary or Conservative Discipline?" *Intercollegiate Review*, 2 (1966), is a helpful analysis of how radical thinkers such as Voltaire have used history to promote their social and political agendas.

[7] Abraham Kuyper, renowned Reformed scholar, expounded on this matter well.

See James Edward McGoldrick, *God's Renaissance Man, the Life and Worl of Abraham Kuyper* (Darlington, UK: Evangelical Press, 2000), pp. 118-20.

[8] For more information about Socinianism, see John C. Godbey, "Fausto and Lelio Sozzini," s. v. *Oxford Encyclopedia of the Reformation*; Lech Szczucki, "Socinianism," Ibid.: David Munroe Cory, *Faustus Socinus* (Boston: Beacon Press, 1932); Zbignieu Ogonowski, "Faustus Socinue," in *Shapers of Religious Traditions in Germany, Switzerland and Poland* 1560-1600, ed., Jill Raitt (New Haven, CT: Yale University Press, 1981), pp. 195-209.

[9] Henry H. Cheethan, *Unitarianism and Universalism: an Illustrated History* (Boston: Beacon Press, 1962) is an excellent introduction. A more thorough effort is that of David Robinson, *The Unitarians and the Universalists* (Westport, CT: Greenwood Press, 1985).

[10] Quoted by ibid., p. 133.

[11] ibid., p. 34.

[12] Joseph Henry Allen, *Our Liberal Movement in Theology* (New York: Arno Press, 1972 reprint of 1892 ed.), p. 35.

[13] ibid., p. 20 (author's emphasis).

[14] Cheetham, *Unitarianism and Universalism*, p. 54.

[15] Allen, *Our Liberal Movement*, pp. 74-106; Robinson, *Unitarianism and Universalism*, 302. Both of these authors endorse Parker's position.

[16] Quoted with approval by Allen, *Our Liberal Movement*, p. 122.

[17] ibid., p. 195.

[18] Robinson, *Unitarianism and Universalism*, p. 145.

[19] Excellent coverage of the pioneer Universalist appears in Ibid. For a brief, critical introduction to Unitarianism and Universalism, see F. E. Mayer, *The Religious Bodies of America* (St. Louis: Concordia Publishing House, 1954), pp. 503-10.

[20] See 77.

[21] Talmage, *Articles of Faith*, p. 29.

[22] ibid., p. 40.

[23] ibid., p. 42.

[24] *Teachings of the Prophet Joseph Smith*, ed., Joseph Fielding Smith (Salt Lake City: Deseret News Press, 1958), p. 370 (emphasis in original).

[25] James Talmage, *Jesus the Christ* (Salt Lake City: Deseret Book Company, 1982 reprint of 1915 ed.), p. 8.

[26] Parley P. Pratt, *Key to Theology*, 9th ed. (Salt Lake City: Deseret Book Company, 1965), pp. 38-39.

[27] ibid., p. 40.

[28] Talmage, *Jesus the Christ*, p. 10. Authoritative current information about the Latter Day Saints appears in the *Encyclopedia of Mormonism*, 5 Vols, ed., Daniel H. Ludlow (New York: Macmillan Publishing Company, 1992).

[29] Charles T. Russell, *The Divine Plan of the Ages* (Brooklyn, NY: The Dawn

Publishers, 1942 reprint of 1886 ed.).

[30] Anthony A. Hoekema, *The Four Major Cults* (Grand Rapids: William B. Eerdmans Publishing Company, 1963), pp. 233-371 has a keen analysis of Russell's ideas.

[31] *Let God be True*, 2nd ed. (Brooklyn, NY: Watchtower Bible and Tract Society, 1956), pp. 18-19.

[32] ibid., p. 100.

[33] *The Greatest Man Who Ever Lived* (Brooklyn, NY: Watchtower Bible and Tract Society, 1991). This remark appears on the fourth page of an introduction without pagination.

[34] ibid.

[35] *Let God be True*, p. 101.

[36] *New World Translation of the Christian Greek Scriptures* (Brooklyn, NY: Watchtower Bible and Tract Society, 1950), p. 282.

[37] *Let God be True*, p. 101.

[38] Jehovah's Witnesses have published a compilation of Bible verses to support their teachings about Christology and other doctrines. The manner in which they have arranged the texts shows habitual disregard for the context of the passages quoted, and it ignores collateral portions of Scripture that shed light on the meaning. Cf. Gordon H. Clark, *The Johannine Logos* (Phillipsburg, NJ: Presbyterian & Reformed Publishing Company, 1972); *Make Sure of all Things* (Brooklyn, NY: Watchtower Bible and Tract Society, 1965).

[39] ibid., p. 282, (emphasis mine).

[40] ibid., p. 283.

[41] *Let God be True*, p. 113.

[42] *Make Sure of all Things*, p. 286.

[43] *Let God be True*, p. 298.

[44] ibid., pp. 298-301.

[45] ibid., p. 276.

[46] A helpful analysis of Watchtower Christology is in Walter R. Martin and Norman H. Klann, *Jehovah of the Watchtower* (New York: Bible Truth Publication Society, 1953), pp. 43-74. See too Hoekema, *Major Cults*, pp. 270-79 and appendix D; and M. James Penton, *Apocalypse Delayed: the Story of Jehovah's Witness* (Toronto: Toronto University Press, 1985). This is a thorough analysis and powerful critique by a former Jehovah's Witness.

[47] Robert Reymond, *The Justification of Knowledge* (Nutley, NJ: Presbyterian & Reformed Publishing Company, 1976), contains an excellent treatment of this matter.

[48] J. Gresham Machen explained this antithesis well in *Christianity and Liberalism* (Grand Rapids: William B. Eerdmans Publishing Company, 1946 reprint of 1923 ed.).

Chapter Four

ANCIENT HERESY: PELAGIANISM

Anthropology

In the Greek Church of the eastern Mediterranean world, fine distinctions of theology held great fascination for scholars, especially disputes about the Trinity and the two natures of Christ. The church there did not, however, show as much interest in the doctrines of anthropology, hamartiology, and soteriology (man, sin and salvation), so the task of clarifying and publishing Christian teaching about those matters occurred in the Latin Church of the West. The most important aspects of these doctrinal issues pertained to the human condition as a consequence of Adam's fall and the role of divine grace and human freedom and responsibility in salvation.

In a work entitled *A Treatise on the Soul* (c. 200), Tertullian set forth the Doctrine of Original Sin, which implies that sinners are helpless to change their depraved condition, but

Tertullian did not perceive the essential implication of this view. He, on the contrary, regarded salvation as dependent upon the decision of the human will, which he said, remains free despite the Fall. Tertullian wrote about God's grace as an infusion of divine aid into the souls of people who work for salvation.[1] His influence was so great that eventually his teaching about salvation became the dominant view in the Middle Ages.

Other theologians, for example, Cyprian (c. 200-58), Bishop of Carthage, and Hilary (c. 315-67), Bishop of Poitiers, wrote about human depravity and contended that baptism of infants is necessary because all people are sinful by nature, due to the transmission of Adam's guilt to his posterity. Ambrose (c. 339-97), Bishop of Milan, one of the great teachers of the Western Church, was a staunch defender of orthodoxy against pagans and Arians, and he maintained that the Fall had produced corruption of human nature which extends to the loss of free will. In his view only divine grace could enable and convince sinners to will to be saved on God's terms.

Pelagianism

The doctrines of anthropology, hamartiology, and soteriology became subjects of intense disputes when Pelagius (c. 350-425), a monk from the British Isles, visited Rome about 390. In the capital city he witnessed much moral laxity among professing Christians, and he realized that leaders of the Latin Church differed from their counterparts in the Greek Church with regard to the state of human nature consequent to the Fall. In the East there was a general consensus that Adam's sin had not deprived sinners of free will, so their salvation was something they initiate by their own volition. The renowned theological school at Alexandria taught this view, and scholars there held that divine grace becomes operative only after people turn to God freely. At that point the assistance of grace enables believers to complete their pilgrimage to eternal life. In contrast to the teachings of Cyprian, Hilary and Ambrose, Pelagius endorsed the Greek doctrine and argued the Latin theology encouraged people to live sinfully. The pessimistic anthropology that stressed the solidarity of the race with Adam in his sin, Pelagius argued, robs people of the incentive to live righteously.

Like some eastern theologians, Pelagius believed each soul is a direct creation of God, and therefore it could not be corrupt from conception. Human nature then is not depraved, and Adam's sin had no profound effects upon his descendents. Pelagius insisted the laws of God imply that humans have freedom and ability to obey them, and it is at least possible to live without sin. Even physical death, he believed, is not a consequence of sin but a natural occurrence. For Pelagius following Christ's example, not dependence on his grace, is the essence of Christian faith. Humans are naturally good, and they sin only by following bad example. Continuing to do so makes sin habitual, but human nature is not corrupt.

Although the teaching of Pelagius echoed the thinking of some Greek theologians, it aroused strong opposition in the Latin West. Where the Eastern Church proclaimed a synergist concept of regeneration in which human decision was paramount, the dominant anthropology in the West featured a conflicting view. Tertullian had advanced the idea of traducianism, the belief that human souls are not individual creations, for humans at conception are complete beings who derive their souls and their bodies from their parents. Theologians after Tertullian deduced from his anthropology the belief that sinful parents produce sinful offspring, so humans have no natural love for God nor any desire to please him.

Following the lead of the Fathers of the Eastern Church, Pelagius maintained a superficial view of sin in that he regarded it as only a mistaken use of the will. His teaching became known while he was in North Africa about 411. In his judgment, sins are particular transgressions not necessarily related to one another and not manifestations of a corrupt nature. Self-control, he thought, is the efficient means to avoid such offenses and to secure salvation.

Pelagius regarded God as primarily a law-giver and Christians as good people with ability to obey him. Pelagius especially disliked the teaching that God holds all human beings accountable for Adam's sin. He understood grace to mean divine revelation and benefits such as forgiveness, but he made the unfettered choice of free will the efficient cause of salvation.

In assessing the importance of Jesus' example, Pelagius viewed the death of Christ as pre-eminently a moral example, and he showed little concern for the ministry of the Holy Spirit, perhaps because he saw no need for regeneration.[2] He lived at a time when mass conversion of pagans was occurring, often due to pressure from civil authorities. As a result, adherence to Christianity was often only a superficial, entirely external conformity that did not produce consistent godly living. Pelagius was appropriately concerned about this state of affairs, but because he failed to understand the moral condition of fallen sinners, his prescription for improvement was unrealistic and grossly inadequate. As his ideas spread, Augustine of Hippo (354-430) emerged as the chief opponent of Pelagius.

Augustine of Hippo

Aurelius Augustinus was the son of a godly mother and a pagan father. Educated in Carthage, the greatest city of Roman North Africa, he learned the wisdom of Greco-Roman culture and demonstrated brilliance as a student of philosophy. Despite his mother Monica's Christian example and fervent prayers, Augustine pursued the path of paganism and espoused its values in his thought and behavior. Philosophy became his passion, as he explored the various schools of thought current at that time. Neo-Platonism made a deep and lasting impression upon him. For a while the teachings of Mani (216-76), a Persian whose father had embraced some Christian concepts through the influence of a Judeo-Christian sect known as the Elkesaites, a rather obscure movement, attracted the interest of Augustine. The Elkesaites claimed direct divine inspiration, as they blended Jewish, Christian and pagan teachings. Mani's understanding of the Christian faith was incomplete and confused, but he became the progenitor of the Manichaean movement which gained a substantial following throughout the Roman Empire in the third century.

Mani traveled extensively to spread his doctrine; he promoted it as the means to unite East and West in a single religion, which included elements of Persian Zoroastrianism and Buddhism, as well as some from Judaism and Christianity. Mani assumed the role of a prophet and founded his own church. Through supposed visions from the Holy Spirit, he claimed to be an "apostle of light." He won some members of the royal court to his sect, but a hostile monarch executed him in 276 and persecuted his followers. Almost destroyed in Persia, the cult's refugees from oppression fled into the Roman Empire. They claimed to be Christians, but bishops of the Eastern Church called them heretics. After the Roman Empire became officially Christian, the government persecuted Manichees, but the sect survived into the sixth century in the West and until the thirteenth century in Central Asia. During the Middle Ages it reappeared to some extent in the teachings of the Paulicians, Bogomils, and Cathars.

Manichaeism featured belief in a radical dualism depicted as a struggle between light and darkness in which astrology was prominent. Manichees held that particles of light surrounded by darkness required liberation to ascend to heaven, and the Milky Way was the ladder by which they climbed in their passage. Cult leaders claimed they could release prisoners of darkness and place them on the path to redemption. They taught that material bodies are prisons which incarcerate particles of light awaiting freedom. Good Christians, they said, refrain from biological reproduction because that would create more prisons.

According to Manichaean doctrine, evil forces had created human bodies, while souls are of heavenly origin. Only those people who joined the Manichaean Church could obtain redemption from the evil material world and ascend to the domain of perfect light. A series of reincarnations would follow until believers gained the status of the elect and the right to enter the realm of eternal light.

The Manichees found a place for Jesus in their teaching by portraying him as the pure spirit of the sun (light) who leads souls out of the material world (darkness), while Satan strives to keep them imprisoned there. There was no divine incarnation, and Jesus had only the appearance of human flesh, not the reality. Manichees contended that the New Testament is a falsified record of Christ's life and teachings and that their prophet Mani had restored the truth of Christianity. History, they maintained, is moving toward a holocaust, when light will triumph over darkness.[3]

As a curious young scholar, Augustine found Manichaeism attractive because it appeared to resolve the problem of the origin of evil, which biblical Christianity does not fully address. He remained with the sect nine years until 383, when he left for Italy. In 385 he became professor of rhetoric in Milan, and there he met Ambrose, the bishop of that city and one of the great preachers and theologians of the ancient church.

Augustine's sojourn in Milan at first involved a study of Neo-Platonism to satisfy his intellect and the practice of fornication to satisfy his lust. He had lived with a concubine thirteen years and had sired a son named Adeodatus, and in Italy he found another paramour. Sexual lust was his compulsion, and yet he found the preaching of Ambrose intriguing, and he attended church services often. The oratory of this bishop fascinated the rhetorician, although he had no intention of accepting Christian doctrine. By placing himself in a position to hear the Word of God, however, the curious scholar became genuinely interested in the teachings of Ambrose as well as his oratorical skill. A conviction of personal sin and the need for forgiveness gradually developed in his mind, and a passage from the pen of the Apostle Paul was the decisive instrument in his conversion. He read,

> let us walk properly, as in the day, not in revelry and drunkenness, not in lewdness and lust, not in strife and envy. But put on the Lord Jesus Christ, and make no provision for the flesh, to fulfill its lusts (Rom. 13:13-14).

Soon Augustine abandoned his worldly ways and became a disciple of Christ. He was baptized in 387.

After returning to Carthage, Augustine became a presbyter and later Bishop of Hippo, where he served until his death. Much of the information about his life comes from Augustine's spiritual autobiography, *The Confessions*, which relates his spiritual, moral, and intellectual struggles and discloses his inclination toward pride and sensuality. This work describes his conversion and refers to all major Christian doctrines, but it is not a systematic presentation of theology or philosophy.

When Monica learned of her son's conversion, having prayed for many years, she rejoiced and expressed her desire to go to heaven. She exclaimed to Augustine:

> *I have no further delight in anything in this life. . . . One thing there was for which I desired to linger for a while. . . , that I might see thee a Catholic Christian. . . . My God hath done this for me more abundantly, that I should now see thee withal, despising earthly happiness, become his servant. What do I here?[4]*

Augustine admitted that lust had long enslaved him, and once he had prayed, "give me chastity. . . , only not yet."[5] When divine grace subdued his evil disposition and enabled him to embrace Christ, he exulted, "by a light as it were of serenity infused into my heart, all the darkness of doubt vanished."[6]

Once a convinced believer, Augustine employed his talent and immense learning in expounding and defending the faith against pagans and heretics. His opposition to Pelagianism was very vigorous, and as a consequence it has become a custom to refer to him as the Doctor (Teacher) of Grace. Like his adversary Pelagius, Augustine had once believed in the free will of fallen sinners, but careful study of Scripture convinced him he was wrong, so he resisted Pelagian doctrine.

Augustine had a profound understanding of original sin and its consequences for the whole human race. He held that pride had led Adam to rebel by using his freedom perversely, and, more emphatically than earlier theologians, the bishop argued that Adam's sin has polluted all of his descendants. Human nature since the fall has been in a corrupt condition in which love of self, rather than love for God, is the dominating principle and the root of all sins. Humans no longer have the freedom Adam enjoyed before the Fall. That is, they are not free not-to-sin, and sin has become their greatest pleasure. The corrupt will is free to choose among sins but does not love God and choose to obey him. Augustine categorically denied the Pelagian contention that it is possible to live without sin.

When he realized some bishops in the East supported the teaching of Pelagius, Augustine resolved to write against it, and for the next twenty years he fought this form of religious humanism. The bishop's initial specifically anti-Pelagian writing was *Concerning the Proceedings of Pelagius*, a treatise from 417, in which he rebuked those prelates who endorsed the false doctrine. His work was an effort to expose the errors of Pelagius after fourteen bishops in Palestine had accepted him as orthodox. In a systematic manner Augustine responded to all major points at issue when his adversary had appeared before the bishops in the Holy Land. The Bishop of Hippo summarized the erroneous soteriology of Pelagius by contending the monk was promoting "a heresy which disputes, under color of defending free will, against the grace of God which we have through our Lord Jesus Christ." He accused Pelagius of teaching "a man can be without sin and keep God's commandments easily if he wishes."[7]

During the next two decades Augustine issued a host of treatises against Pelagian doctrine and convinced leaders of the church to renounce them officially. Synods of bishops in North Africa condemned the errors, and they persuaded Innocent I (402-17), Bishop of Rome, to endorse their position. Soon, however, Innocent died, and Zosimus (417-18) succeeded him. The new Bishop of Rome, who appears to have come from the East, had little knowledge of theology, and he soon entertained an appeal from the Pelagian faction and reversed the condemnation of his predecessor. Augustine and other leaders turned for support to Roman Emperor Honorius (395-423), who condemned the teaching of Pelagius and ordered banishment for people who promoted it. Under imperial pressure, Bishop Zosimus relented and approved the censure which North African bishops had pronounced at Carthage in 418. The next two Bishops of Rome, Boniface I (418-22) and Celestine (422-32), were resolutely opposed to Pelagianism, and the Council of Ephesus (431) condemned it.

Official rejection of false teaching never assures its demise, and Pelagianism continued to agitate controversy long after its primary teacher died. Augustine therefore wrote extensively to combat its ongoing influence. In 427, for example, he issued his treatise *Concerning Grace and Free Will*,[8] in which he affirmed the biblical doctrines of original sin, election to salvation, and perseverance in the faith, and he attributed salvation entirely to the grace of God without regard for merit or any human contribution.

Death removed Augustine from the arena of theological controversy in 430, but disputes about salvation continued, and a school of Semi-Pelagian thought arose in Gaul, where John Cassian (c. 365-433), a leading monk-theologian, challenged Augustinian teaching about soteriology. He contended that God's grace is a response to human initiative, as people turn to God by the decision of their free will.

Cassian had spent time in Constantinople, where he absorbed ideas about synergism and where he developed a fondness for the rigorous asceticism of Egyptian monks.

The view that grace is a divinely bestowed aid to people who will to be saved denies the depravity of fallen human nature by affirming the ability of sinners to seek God by their own volition. It negates the biblical diagnosis of the human condition as one of spiritual death (Eph. 2:1), by insisting that sinners have a native capacity to co-operate with God's grace by taking the first step in gaining salvation.

Semi-Pelagian soteriology won substantial acceptance, but the influence of Augustine was sufficient to lead the church to condemn it officially, even though some scholars argued that it was the teaching of most of the ancient Church Fathers. Defenders of Semi-Pelagianism claimed Augustine was an innovator whose beliefs did not reflect the historic Christian position regarding sin and salvation. Vincent of Lerins (d. c. 445), a monk from Gaul, contested the teaching of Augustine, although he did not name the Bishop of Hippo in his polemics. He and Faustus, Bishop of Riez in Provence (d. c. 490), argued for the priority of unfettered human choice in salvation, and thereby they collided with the staunch monergism of Augustine's teaching. Faustus wrote *Concerning the Grace of God and Free Will*, in which he claimed the first step in salvation, the act of faith, must be a human initiative. To Vincent and Faustus, predestination meant the decision to accept people God foreknows will choose him, a view which makes human, rather than divine, choice ultimate.

Augustine published *The Predestination of the Saints* and *The Gift of Perseverance* to rebut the arguments of Cassian and other early Semi-Pelagians, but the great North African theologian died before the church could take an official position regarding the dispute. That occurred at the Synod of Orange in 529. This assembly met in Gaul under the presidency of Caesar, Bishop of Arles (470-542), who defended the broad outlines, but not all of the particulars of Augustine's doctrine. The synod adopted twenty-five canons which reject Semi-Pelagianism and extol salvation by grace alone. These pronouncements uphold Augustine's teachings about human depravity and the loss of a genuinely free will, and they declare that saving faith is an undeserved gift from God. The canons do not, however, address the doctrine of predestination, except to deny that God has predestined anyone to hell.

Boniface II (530-32), Bishop of Rome, approved the decision of Orange, and after 530 Semi-Pelagianism was regarded as heresy, but the church did not endorse the soteriology of Augustine in its entirety. Orange emphasized baptism as the primary means of regenerating grace, which empowers believers to do all that God requires for salvation. This ambiguity encouraged the growing popularity of Tertullian's concept *infused grace* as the means which enables people to perform meritorious good works. As a consequence, a synergistic understanding of salvation continued to enjoy acceptance, and in the Middle Ages the Augustinian doctrines of grace were eclipsed as belief in the efficacy of human merit became the most widely accepted view of salvation. A vigorous resurgence of Augustinian doctrine did not occur until the Protestant Reformation in the sixteenth century, even though there were occasional but unsuccessful efforts to promote it in medieval times.[9]

Modern Counterparts:
Roman Catholicism and Arminianism

In a park in Geneva, Switzerland, stands a large monument

that honors the contributions of the Protestant reformers to the rediscovery of biblical teaching after centuries of false doctrine. Inscribed on that memorial are the words *Post Tenebrae, Lux* —After Darkness, Light. A careful study of church history reveals that the darkness in question featured a false and harmful understanding of sin and salvation, one with conspicuously Semi-Pelagian elements. Beginning with Martin Luther (1483-1546), Protestant Bible scholars tested the teachings of the medieval church against the plain declarations of Scripture and found many of them to be untrue. In the centuries since the Synod of Orange renounced it as heresy, Semi-Pelagianism had become the unofficial but predominant soteriology of the church, East and West. The light of the gospel of free grace had been almost extinguished because the church had neglected to maintain her historic Pauline-Augustinian position. A concept of works-righteousness was central in the church, and professing Christians thought of grace as an infusion of divine assistance that made it possible for them to earn eternal life. A synergistic, legalistic religion had replaced the faith of the Apostles, but in the providence of God, light was again to shine brightly, as Martin Luther, Ulrich Zwingli, Martin Bucer, John Calvin and others studied the Bible and found there the truth of *sola gratia* — salvation by grace alone. That is, a free, unmerited gift from God.

Roman Catholic Pelagianism

The transition from the theology of grace to a system of works-righteousness occurred gradually, but by the late Middle Ages few teachers in the Roman Church had a clear perception of biblical teaching about sin and salvation. When the Protestant reformers found the truth of *sola gratia*, their proclamations appeared to be radical innovations, and the established church condemned them as heresies. The reformers replied by supporting their assertions from Scripture and by citing St Augustine as their predecessor in the ancient church. Many of the writings of sixteenth century Protestant scholars abound with references to the Bishop of Hippo, whom the reformers regarded as indeed the Doctor (Teacher) of Grace.[10] They argued that Wittenburg, Zurich, Geneva, and other seats of Evangelical learning were preserving the genuine Catholic faith, while Rome and its universities were promoting Semi-Pelagian falsehood.

As the Roman Church witnessed the spread of Protestantism, it responded to the challenge by assuming a posture of militant defensiveness, and it resolved to make no concessions to its opponents. A Counter-Reformation began as a means to thwart the Evangelical movement, as Rome raised medieval theology to the status of dogma-teaching that is mandatory for all to believe.

In line with earlier papal pronouncements, the Church of Rome presented herself as the fountain of saving grace to which sinners must resort for forgiveness. Only her priests could dispense the grace of God, and submission to the authority of Rome was essential. As Pope Boniface VIII (1294-1303) declared in the bull *Unam Sanctam* (1302), "it is altogether necessary to salvation for every human creature to be subject to the Roman pontiff."[11] The multitudes who accepted such teachings came to rely chiefly upon the church rather than upon Christ for salvation, and the church sought alliances with civil authorities to enforce its prescriptions. It encouraged the belief that salvation is a reward for obedience to ecclesiastical authority, and performing stipulated moral and ceremonial duties is the essence of Christian faith. It is evident that the Latin Church of the West had accepted the anthropology of the Greek Church in the East and had forsaken the Augustinian heritage.

Counter-Reformation-Catholicism's denial of total depravity and its espousal of salvation by grace plus works remains its doctrine today, so modern Catholicism is Semi-Pelagian. Rome insists that grace is *essential* for salvation but denies it is *sufficient* to save sinners. Roman Catholic worship features an elaborate system of sacraments under the control of the priesthood, and a conspicuous clergy-laity, sacred-secular dichotomy makes everyone dependent upon the church for saving grace. In Roman teaching baptism is the regenerating sacrament which cleanses original sin and all other sins committed prior to baptism. Penance forgives post-baptismal sins, as people confess to their priests and receive absolution. Other sacraments impart divine aid for a life of meritorious good works.

The climax of the Counter-Reformation came with the pronouncements of the Council of Trent (1545-63), in which Jesuit influence was paramount. Founded by Ignatius Loyola (1491-1556), a former soldier in the service of Spain, the Society of Jesus became the vanguard of the Roman offensive against Protestant heretics. Loyola was both a scholar and a mystic whose devotion to Catholicism was unexcelled. Well-educated theologians of his movement became advisors to the Vatican, and their militant hatred for Protestantism is evident in the decisions of Trent, which the pope eventually declared dogma. The major declarations of Trent as they relate to salvation include a reaffirmation of the entire sacramental system as it had developed during the Middle Ages and a clear declaration on soteriology. At its fifth session the council asserted that baptism cleanses recipients from original sin and accomplishes the regeneration of sinful souls. In the sixth session it proclaimed original sin does not deprive fallen sinners of free will, so they retain some ability to "convert themselves to their own justification by freely assenting to and cooperating with . . . grace."[12] In accord with this teaching, Trent declared that no one can be justified without baptism. Which is the "instrumental cause." Although justification proceeds from the grace of God conferred through baptism, justification does not produce only a *declared* righteousness imputed to believers through faith. It actually *makes* them righteous "according to each one's disposition and cooperation." There is in justification an *infusion* of virtues, principally faith, hope and charity.[13]

Because the canons of Trent assert a synergistic view of salvation, they necessarily deny that believers may enjoy assurance, "since no one can know with the certainty of faith, ... that he has obtained the grace of God."[14] Although there is a chapter of the canons which acknowledges the reality of predestination, it states that to claim certainty about election is sinful presumption, except in rare instances when God may disclose that to a person through a special revelation.[15]

While the documents of Trent refer often to the indispensability of God's grace for salvation, they, at the same time, assign saving significance to human merit and reject the belief that justification is an act of God's free grace to which there is no human contribution. The precise statements concerning justification declare:

> *If anyone says that men are justified either by the sole imputation of the justice [righteousness] of Christ or by the sole remission of sins, to the exclusion of the grace and charity which is poured forth in their hearts by the Holy Ghost, or that the grace by which [people] are justified is only the good will of God, let him be anathema [accursed].*
>
> *If anyone says that justifying faith is nothing else than confidence*

*in divine mercy, which remits sins for Christ's sake, or that it is
confidence alone that justifies, ... let him be anathema.*

*If anyone says that the justice [righteousness] received is not
preserved and not increased before God through good works, but that
those works are merely the fruits and signs of justification obtained,
but not the cause of its increase, let him be anathema.*

*If anyone says that, after the reception of the grace of justification
the guilt is so remitted and the debt of eternal punishment so blotted
out to every penitent sinner, that no debt of temporal punishment
remains to be discharged, either in this world or in purgatory, before
the gates of heaven can be opened, let him be anathema.*[16]

The documents from Trent show clearly that the Roman
Catholic Church, despite its formal condemnation of Pelagian
and Semi-Pelagian doctrines, does not espouse salvation *sola
gratia* – by grace alone. It, on the contrary, affirms a version
of Semi-Pelagianism in which human merit is a necessary
component of its soteriology. The decisions of Trent hold the
status of dogma, which is not subject to change. Although
some contemporary scholars of the Roman Church may
be attracted to a monergistic view of salvation, the official
position of their church remains synergistic, as an examination
of current Catholic publications will demonstrate.

The most authoritative recent manual of Roman teachings
is the *Catechism of the Catholic Church*, which appeared in 1994,
and to which the Vatican holds the copyright.[17] In explaining
the church's position on sin and salvation, the catechism
denies the total depravity of sinners by asserting that original
sin has caused "a deprivation of original holiness and justice
[righteousness], but human nature has not been totally
corrupted: it is wounded in the natural powers proper to it."
Baptism is the approved remedy for this condition because it
imparts the grace which "erases original sin and turns a man
back toward God."[18] In teaching that sin has *wounded* human

beings, the catechism does not recognize the mortal gravity of sin, which Scripture states has produced spiritual *death* (Eph. 2:1; Col. 2:13). It is true the catechism refers to original sin as leading to "the death of the soul,"[19] but it does not for that reason conclude that fallen humans are in a helpless condition of inability to please and satisfy God. According to Roman Catholic doctrine, the Fall did not deprive sinners of a truly free will, and "by free will one shapes one's own life."[20] The possession of freedom, "especially in moral and religious matters, is an inalienable requirement of the dignity of the human person."[21]

The *Catechism of the Catholic Church* does admit that sin has impaired human freedom and that persistent sinning produces a condition of servitude to sin, but this manual of doctrine does not conclude that the human state is one of helpless bondage to evil in which people lack both the will and the ability to love God and to avoid sin. The catechism declares instead that Christ's sacrificial death "has won salvation for all men. He redeemed them from the sin that held them in bondage." Taken literally, this statement appears to teach universal "liberation and salvation,"[22] for those are the terms the manual employs. Further reading will show, however, that this is not the teaching of the Roman Church. It does hold, nevertheless, that sinners must co-operate with God's grace in order to be saved and they have the ability to do so, in spite of their moral and spiritual condition. This contention perpetuates a Semi-Pelagian view of salvation.

Reading the *Catechism of the Catholic Church* with comprehension requires careful concentration, because much of its language is evangelical, and some of its declarations about soteriology appear to be biblical. This is particularly so with regard to the matter of justification. Beginning with

Martin Luther, the Protestant reformers were resolute in proclaiming justification by grace alone through faith alone in Christ alone, and their position put them at odds with the Roman Church, as the decisions of Trent already cited show clearly. The reformers maintained that the faith by which believers receive forgiveness and salvation is an unmerited gift from God, and the catechism agrees by stating, "faith is a supernatural gift from God. In order to believe, man needs the interior helps of the Holy Spirit."[23] The catechetical definition of faith includes assent to divine revelation, as the Holy Spirit "moves the heart" and enables people to accept the truth.[24] This faith is essential for salvation, and "without faith no one has ever attained justification."[25] Moreover, justification is a fruit of grace which God grants freely to undeserving sinners "to respond to his call to become children of God, adopted sons, partakers of the divine nature and of eternal life."[26]

Were this the entire Catholic doctrine of justification, Protestants would not dissent, but more is involved. For example, Rome presents baptism as the means of justification because it is "the sacrament of faith." In support of this assertion the catechism cites Romans 3:21-26, a passage which does not mention baptism, but one which clearly states that God justifies "him who has faith in Jesus." The Apostle Paul, in this text, was emphatic in declaring justification occurs "apart from the law" (3:21). That is, it is not due to any act or work humans might perform in obedience to the law of God. It is a work *of God* on behalf of believing sinners by which the righteousness of God becomes the possession of believers through faith in Christ. Since faith is a gift from God (Eph. 2:8-9), as is regeneration, there is no human contribution to justification, which is a monergistic achievement.

Contrary to the New Testament teaching about justification

by grace alone, the Catholic Church presents it as a synergistic accomplishment, and here the exact words of the catechism merit careful attention.

> *Justification establishes co-operation between God's grace and man's freedom. On man's part it is expressed by the assent of faith to the Word of God, which invites him to conversion, and in the co-operation of charity with the prompting of the Holy Spirit, who precedes and preserves his assent.*[27]

In order to support the above contention, the catechism does not quote Scripture but rather a pronouncement from the Council of Trent.

From a biblical point of view, the most objectionable feature of the Roman Catholic position regarding justification is the role it assigns to human merit. Like earlier theologians reaching back as far as Tertullian, the compilers of the *Catechism of the Catholic Church* promote the concept of *infused grace*. This doctrine proceeds from the assumption that Christ entrusted the church with a repository of grace (supernatural assistance) from which it can dispense aid to needy sinners who seek it. This infusion of grace then empowers believers to perform works of merit and thereby to participate synergistically in the work of salvation.

> *Grace, by uniting us in active love, ensures the supernatural quality of our acts and consequently their merit before God and before men. The saints have always had a lively awareness that their merits were pure grace.*[28]

The authority for this pronouncement is St Therese of Lisieux (1873-97), a Carmelite nun from France.

Although the catechism repeatedly declares divine grace to be essential for human merit, it nevertheless presents such merit as a necessary part of justification. "Merit is to be ascribed in the first place to the grace of God, secondly to man's collaboration. Man's merit is due to God."[29]

The rather confusing Roman Catholic view of salvation is due in some measure to that church's failure to distinguish adequately between justification and sanctification. Justification has long been the subject of debate among professing Christians, and this has been due in large part to the term itself. *Justification* is a combination of two Latin words, *justus*, which means *just* or *righteous*, and *facere*, the verb *to make*. In theology this term describes the way in which believing sinners acquire right standing with God. The difficulty in understanding this matter is because the Latin term does not adequately convey the meaning of the Greek one in the New Testament, where the word is *dikaio*, which means *to declare just* or *righteous* (Rom. 5:1; 8:30-33; Gal. 2:16; 3:11). The compilers of the *Westminster Shorter Catechism* (1647) understood this to mean that God *imputes* the perfect righteousness of Christ to regenerated sinners who believe the gospel and receive Christ through faith. Hence the Presbyterian catechism, in contrast with its Catholic counterpart, declares:

> *Justification in an act of God's free grace, wherein he pardons all our sins, and accepts us as righteous in his sight, only for the righteousness of Christ imputed to us and received by faith alone.*[30]

Historic Protestantism emphasizes that, in justification, the term *imputation* means God reckons or accounts to believing, penitent sinners the flawless righteousness of Christ. It is the Savior's righteousness alone which makes sinners acceptable to God, since they cannot produce the perfect righteousness God demands. In other words, the righteousness God requires God himself supplies. The *Westminster Confession of Faith* (1647), in chapter XI is precise in stating that justification does not involve *infusing righteousness* into sinners, but "accounting and accepting their persons as righteous; not for anything wrought in them, but for Christ's sake alone." Whereas Roman Catholics portray justification as a co-operative endeavor, Protestants stress its monergistic character as *sola gratia* – a work of grace alone.

Protestants who define justification as the imputation of believers' sins to Christ, and of his righteousness to them, often encounter the charge that this teaching promotes lax morality and discourages good works. This misunderstanding, too, is due to a failure to distinguish sufficiently between justification and sanctification. In response to this criticism, the *Westminster Confession of Faith* adds to its statement about justification:

> *faith thus receiving and resting on Christ and his righteousness, is the alone [only] instrument of justification: yet it is not alone in the person justified, but is ever accompanied with all other saving graces, is no dead faith, but works by love.*

Sanctification is another Latin term. *Sanctus* means *holy*, and *facere* is *to make*. Once more the Presbyterian confession is precise in its definition by showing that sinners justified through faith alone in Christ alone are:

> *sanctified, really and personally, through the virtue of Christ's death and resurrection, by his Word and Spirit dwelling in them: the dominion of the whole body of sin is destroyed, and the several lusts thereof are more and more weakened and mortified; and they more and more quickened [enlivened] and strengthened in all saving graces, to the practice of true holiness, without which no man shall see the Lord.* [31]

In sanctification, justified sinners, as believers in Christ, pursue lives of righteousness and holiness by obeying the laws of

God, as his grace enables them. Rather than encourage laxity, the proper understanding of justification and sanctification leads to a desire for godliness, as the Apostle Paul indicated in his letter to Titus:

> the grace of God that brings salvation has appeared to all men, teaching us that, denying ungodliness and worldly lusts, we should live soberly, righteously, and godly in the present age, looking for the blessed hope and glorious appearing of our great God and Savior Jesus Christ, who gave himself for us, that he might redeem us from every lawless deed and purify for himself his own special people, zealous for good works (2:11-14).

Although justification by grace alone through faith alone in Christ alone excludes the possibility of any meritorious human contribution, it inspires the beneficiaries of this grace to perform good works zealously, as a way to show gratitude to God for his saving intervention in their lives. The dispute between Roman Catholics and Protestants is not about the *necessity* for grace but the *sufficiency* of grace in salvation. Scripture proclaims salvation, in its entirety, as a gift from God. The *Catechism of the Catholic Church*, on the other hand, insists upon the contribution of human merit. In Semi-Pelagian fashion, Catholicism makes salvation, in some measure, contingent upon the works of man. The Gospel, however, presents a Christ who actually saves sinners by his work alone. An angel informed Joseph, "you shall call his name Jesus, for he shall save his people from their sins" (Matt. 1:21). If people could save themselves, or if they could do something deserving of salvation, Jesus Christ would not be the Savior. A correct understanding of soteriology requires the proper distinction between justification and sanctification. It is a serious error to confuse them, and it is an equally grave mistake to divorce

139

them. Paul, in affirming the gratuitous nature of salvation, was quick to show that it produces wholesome results in the good works of believers. He wrote:

> *it is by grace you have been saved, through faith — and this not from yourselves, it is the gift of God — not by works, so that no one can boast. For we are God's workmanship, created in Christ Jesus to do good works, which God prepared in advance for us to do (Eph. 2:8-10, NIV, emphasis mine).*

Since the pronouncements of Trent are among the dogmas of Roman Catholicism, it should surprise no one that the Catholic catechism cites them often as its authority. While it is evident that the Church of Rome has softened its attitude toward Protestants and no longer denounces them as heretics, its synergistic doctrine of salvation remains, as the affirmations of Vatican Council II (1962-65) demonstrate.[32] Protestants, in contrast, continue to maintain, as Luther contended, that justification *sola fide* — through faith alone, is the article by which the church will stand or fall.[33] In the Smalcald Articles (1537) Luther wrote about justification by grace alone through faith alone. He said, "nothing in this article can be given up or compromised, even if heaven and earth and things temporal should be destroyed."[34] The great reformer was adamant because he knew there could be no gospel without this truth, but the Church of Rome disagrees and continues to extol the value of human merit in obtaining acceptance with God. As one Protestant analyst of Vatican Council II has remarked,

> *Man still instinctively wants to trust in what he is and does and believes. The church indeed had officially repudiated rank Pelagianism at the ... Council of Ephesus in 431 and at the Synod of Orange in 529, yet the essential error of this heresy infiltrated into her teaching*

> ... *and did much to corrupt and weaken life in Jesus Christ. Martin*
> *Luther and other reformers opposed a type of Semi-Pelagianism which*
> *was later officially approved by the Council of Trent.*[35]

Martin Luther himself succinctly explained the Protestant view of salvation in his *Small Catechism*:

> *I believe that I cannot by my own reason or strength believe in Jesus*
> *Christ, my Lord, or come to him; but the Holy Spirit has called me by*
> *the Gospel, enlightened me with his gifts, sanctified me and kept me in*
> *the true faith; even as he calls, gathers, enlightens, and sanctifies the*
> *whole Christian Church on earth, and keeps it with Jesus Christ in the*
> *one true faith.*[36]

The contrast between biblical teaching and synergistic Semi-Pelagianism is clear, and the Roman Church espouses the latter, not the former.

Arminianism, The Protestant Semi-Pelagianism

The firm Protestant response to the papal church in the sixteenth century included publication of confessions of faith to rebut Semi-Pelagian doctrines that Rome had chosen to maintain. Within only a few years after Luther protested the sale of indulgences in 1517, his church and other Protestant bodies assumed a strongly anti-Pelagian posture. The *Augsburg Confession of Faith* (1530) quickly became the doctrinal statement for almost all Lutheran churches, and its monergistic declarations reflect determined opposition to any and all denials of salvation *sola gratia*.[37] In 1524-25 Luther engaged the leading Catholic humanist Desiderius Erasmus (1466-1536) in a published debate about these issues, and Luther's book *The Bondage of the Will* became the classical Protestant treatise defending divine sovereignty against the

Semi-Pelagian contentions of late medieval Catholicism, as Erasmus asserted them.

As the Reformation spread, other Protestant leaders joined the effort to combat synergistic views of salvation and to exalt the power of God's grace. Among proponents of *sola gratia, sola fide* were Ulrich Zwingli (1484-1531), John Calvin (1509-64), William Tyndale (c. 1495-1536), John Knox (1514-72). Although these reformers differed among themselves about some questions of doctrine, they were united in opposition to synergism, whatever its source. The objectionable soteriology appeared in non-Catholic circles by 1525, as Anabaptists rejected Protestant teaching and proclaimed a view which is closer to Roman Catholicism than to either the Lutheran or the Reformed position.[38] There was a general rejection of total depravity among the Anabaptists and an almost uniform belief in free will. Protestants as well as Catholics regarded Anabaptists as heretics and often wrote to expose their errors. Persecution of these sects was common in Europe, more in Roman Catholic than Protestant lands, since both camps regarded them as subversives, enemies of church and state.

Jacob Arminius

While the challenge of Anabaptism disturbed the major Protestant reformers, the appearance of Semi-Pelagianism within their own ranks was even more alarming. A particularly dramatic expression of this development appeared in the Netherlands due to the defection of Jacob Arminius (1560-1609) from Reformed theology. Arminius, a minister of the Dutch Reformed Church, became a professor of theology at the University of Leyden in 1603. He had studied in Geneva and had been a noteworthy pastor in Amsterdam. As a Reformed minister, he subscribed to the *Belgic Confession of Faith* (1561), a staunchly Calvinistic statement of doctrine.

While serving on a theological commission for his church, Arminius began to reveal his doubts about some aspects of Reformed soteriology, especially predestination. While still a pastor in Amsterdam, he wrote but did not publish a number of treatises that contradict the Reformed position on sin and salvation, and he expressed his disapproval of the teachings of Calvin and Theodore Beza (1516-1605), Calvin's successor as chief pastor in Geneva. Despite his reluctance to leave Amsterdam, and some opposition to his appointment at the university, Arminius joined the faculty in Leyden.

Since he had already aroused suspicions about his subscription to the Reformed faith, Arminius began his academic career in an atmosphere of contention. His major critic was Franz Gomarus (1563-1641), who had been a professor at Leyden since 1594. Gomarus and other Reformed leaders suspected Arminius was a Pelagian and perhaps a Socinian. Before assuming his post, Arminius was required to submit to an examination for the Doctor of Theology degree, and during that exercise it appears he was less than forthright in revealing his beliefs, which, evidence now shows, were out of harmony with the official teaching of his church. Gomarus kept the new professor under scrutiny, and by late 1604 disputes between them had become acrimonious, especially their conflicting views of predestination. In order to promote his deviations from Reformed orthodoxy and to gain acceptance for them, Arminius sought revisions of the two major doctrinal standards of the Dutch Reformed Church, which are the *Belgic Confession* and the *Heidelberg Catechism* (1563). This effort did not succeed, but the controversy it provoked continued long after Arminius died. Some of his followers formed a faction which resolved to achieve the aims of their mentor, and they proposed that the Dutch Reformed Church consider the changes Arminius had desired. The formal request for revisions in doctrine appeared in the Remonstrance of 1610, but the church did not convene a national synod to decide the issues until 1618, a conclave now known as the Synod of Dort. The Remonstrant and Counter-Remonstrant parties contended for control of the Dutch Reformed Church after Arminius died, and Gomarus was the leading theologian of the faction opposed to Arminian teachings.

The Synod of Dort

Efforts to reconcile Arminius and Gomarus while both were teaching at Leyden failed, and two years after the death of his opponent, Gomarus left the university. He was a pastor for a brief time and then a professor in France before he joined the faculty of the University of Groningen, a stronghold of Calvinism in the northern Netherlands. When the church met at Dort, Gomarus led the successful effort to condemn Arminian doctrine. The Synod was in session for six months, and Reformed leaders from several countries attended. Thirteen theologians represented the Remonstrant position, with Simon Episcopius (1583-1634), a professor from Leyden, as their leader. After five weeks of contentious debates, the assembly dismissed the Arminians and proceeded to compose and publish the *Canons of Dort*, or *Five Articles Against the Remonstrants* as clarifications of the *Belgic Confession*. The *Canons* together with the *Confession* and the *Heidelberg Catechism* soon became the *Three Forms of Unity*, the official documents of the Dutch Reformed Church. The decisions at Dort affirmed a strict, robust Calvinist theology, and they encouraged Reformed believers in other lands to maintain their faith undiluted in the face of various challenges.

Although the Dutch government banished the Arminian leaders, it soon allowed them to return, and they established a seminary in Amsterdam which enabled them to spread their doctrine through much of Europe. In the eighteenth century Arminianism made great gains in Britain through the work of John and Charles Wesley, and since then Arminian soteriology has been in the ascendancy throughout Christendom, in spite of occasional revivals of the Reformed faith. The Arminian emphasis is upon personal religious experience rather than doctrine, and that has encouraged subjective beliefs and emotional expressions of such beliefs, as in the charismatic movement.[39]

There can be no doubt that the doctrines of Jacob Arminius conflicted sharply with the theology of the Reformation, Lutheran and Reformed, and the discrepancy is particularly evident in their divergent understanding of sin and salvation. Because he denied the Protestant teaching about total depravity, Arminius could and did espouse a Semi-Pelagian view of soteriology. He maintained the Fall did not deprive sinners of free will and the consequent ability to co-operate with God in salvation. In his view, grace enables people to make a free choice of Christ, but grace is not irresistible; humans may refuse grace. God has foreseen those who will choose Christ and has elected them for salvation on the basis of their foreseen faith. Writing in 1602, Arminius argued:

> The salvation of free will by grace involves the choice of the free will, or else the free will could not be said to be saved... By an absolute predestination God wills to save those who believe and to damn those who persevere in disobedience; by a conditional predestination God wills to save those individuals whom he foresees as believing and persevering and to damn those whom he sees as not believing.[40]

Like preceding Semi-Pelagians, Arminius and his disciples insisted upon the necessity of divine grace for salvation, but they contended that free will co-operation makes grace effectual. They therefore rejected the doctrines of unconditional election and particular redemption, and they expressed doubts about the Reformed confidence in the perseverance of believers unto eternity. Some of the Remonstrants were bolder and more dogmatic in their attacks upon Reformed theology than their tutor had been, and all of them made human choice the ultimate factor in election. Their evident synergism is therefore more compatible with Catholicism than with historic Protestantism.

Although early Remonstrants sought to maintain a broadly evangelical theology, their denial of total depravity and their insistence upon free will led eventually to a humanistic conception of Christianity. Their seminary in Amsterdam became liberal to the point that Socinian-Unitarian teachings were acceptable there. When the Dutch Reformed Church began sending missionaries to the East Indies, it was not the Arminians, but the strict Calvinists who led the way. The leader of overseas evangelism was Petrus Plancius (1552-1622), a staunch advocate of Reformed theology, who was the first prominent critic of Jacob Arminius.[41]

Post-Reformation Arminianism in Britain

The stern rejection of Arminian teachings by the Dutch Reformed Church did not eliminate it in the Netherlands, nor did it prevent the spread of that doctrine to other countries. Anabaptists had preceded the Arminians in accepting Semi-Pelagian principles, and they were widely dispersed across Europe long before the Remonstrants challenged the Reformed faith. The scholarship of Arminius and some of his associates did, however, give their version of Semi-

Pelagianism more credibility than that of the Anabaptists.

Concurrent with the Arminian dispute in the Netherlands, Puritanism was becoming prominent in England, where the Church of England had adopted the *Thirty-Nine Articles of Religion* (1571). This document contains a clear affirmation of Reformed soteriology, to which the Puritans subscribed heartily, but the reform of the Anglican Church had not progressed sufficiently to satisfy rigorous Protestants for whom too much Catholic ritual remained. Since the Church of England was the religion established by law any conflicts about doctrine or liturgy necessarily involved the monarch and parliament. During the reign of Charles I (1625-49) Arminian beliefs within the established church became evident at the same time that ritualistic forms of worship in the manner of the Catholic Church were gaining acceptance. The king was resolved to advance the cause of Arminianism and ritualism, and to promote those developments; he appointed William Laud (1573-1645) Archbishop of Canterbury in 1633. This determined opponent of Calvinism ignored the *Thirty-Nine Articles* and worked to achieve an Anglo-Catholic Church of England. Many Puritans suspected Laud was a crypto-Roman Catholic, but the king made his archbishop his chief advisor in political as well as religious affairs. Laud methodically moved other Arminians into positions of authority within the Anglican Church, while Charles ruled in an arbitrary, almost despotic, manner to the great aggravation of the parliament.

Puritan Resistance

Political issues and contention about taxation were prominent factors in controversies between the crown and parliament, but religion excited much passion, as the king and the archbishop tried to nullify many of the changes which had come to England as results of her Protestant Reformation. The Puritans, who criticized the king's policy, sometimes suffered cruel persecution in the way of fines, imprisonment, even physical mutilation. Laud dismissed pastors who did not co-operate with his scheme, and he prosecuted dissenters who conducted non-Anglican worship. These measures aroused a large majority of Englishmen to resist their monarch. Charles and Laud had divided the realm religiously and politically into opposing camps with no middle ground between them.

The authoritarian actions of state and church extended to Scotland too, over which Charles was also king. He and Laud decided to require the Church of Scotland to conform to their designs for the Church of England by ordering the use of the Anglican *Book of Common Prayer* and by imposing bishops to govern the Scottish church. Most Scottish Protestants were Presbyterians by conviction and so resented the royal policy, which they determined to oppose. The Scots denied the king's claim to divine-right monarchy over church and state, and they bound themselves together by a National Covenant to defend their Calvinist faith and Presbyterian form of church government, both of which Charles despised. A Scottish army confronted the king's force at the English border, and the intimidated ruler withdrew. The Scots held aloft a banner with the words *For Christ's Crown and Covenant*. Charles then sought aid from the English Parliament, but he encountered fierce opposition there. Civil war erupted in England in 1642, so Charles could not make war on the Scots, who then supported the army of the English Parliament in its resistance to the crown. Scottish Presbyterians and English Puritans agreed to reform both kingdoms by removing the hated bishops, eliminating residual elements of Romanism, and by affirming Christ's kingship over all.

The Westminster Assembly (1643-48)

On June 12, 1643 the English Parliament summoned an assembly to reform the liturgy of the Anglican Church, to revise its confession, and to promote unity with the Scots and with Reformed churches on the continent. The assembly at Westminster was to advise parliament in ecclesiastical matters. The Church of Scotland sent eight commissioners after parliament subscribed to the Solemn League and Covenant of 1638, and Scottish influence was decisive in the proceedings, though Scots were there in only an advisory role. Even though some members of the Westminster Assembly were Episcopalians and others Independents, the majority supported the Presbyterian position on church polity, and the assembly adopted a new confession, and a directory for worship. All participants at Westminster agreed that they should purge England of Arminian and Roman Catholic teachings, and parliament approved the documents the assembly produced. Although the Westminster Assembly was a major triumph for Protestantism, its influence was to be stronger and more lasting in Scotland than in England.

The details of the English Civil War (1642-49) are beyond the scope of the present study, but it is important to note that the conflict led to the execution of Charles I, abolition of the monarchy, and armed conflict between Englishmen and Scots, as the king attempted to divide and conquer his enemies. The Scots desired to restrict the ruler's powers and to protect their liberty in religion, but they did not seek to terminate the monarchy. A broad spectrum of English Puritans, however, wanted to be rid of the crown forever, and many of them were Independents who opposed Presbyterian church polity. Although Charles beguiled the Scots by claiming he would accept Presbyterianism, his Scottish army suffered defeat, as Oliver Cromwell led the English to victory. The English Parliament then expelled its Presbyterian members and executed the king.

Cromwell, as Lord Protector (1649-58), inflicted more defeats upon the Scots and thereby became ruler of Scotland, which he governed in an authoritarian way, although he protected it against Catholicism and allowed Presbyterians to minister freely. England was without a king until the restoration of 1660 brought Charles II (1660-85) to the throne. After the return of the monarchy, the Church of England retained the *Thirty-Nine Articles*, Episcopal government, and the *Book of Common Prayer*. The church was still officially Reformed in doctrine, but there was a diminishing interest in preserving its theology, as Puritan influence waned. The Anglican Church gradually became elastic to the point that it tolerated a broad diversity of beliefs while remaining uniform in liturgy and polity. Christians who regarded sound doctrine as essential for a true church moved into Congregational and Baptist churches.

An Act of Uniformity (1662) required all Anglican pastors to accept the approved liturgy or lose their positions, and about 1760 ministers of Puritan persuasion were expelled from their parishes and deprived of their incomes. The growth of Semi-Pelagian-Arminian teaching in the Church of England led that body away from its Reformation heritage and produced a broad church in which no one is required to subscribe to its historic confession. Anglicans today consider their clergymen priests, and they ordain women and seek ecumenical relations with other churches, Roman Catholic, Eastern Orthodox and Protestant, regardless of the doctrines those bodies teach. Having forsaken the principles of the Reformation, the Church of England and its Episcopal associates, with some exceptions, have become

Catholic rather than Protestant. The gift shop in St Paul's Cathedral, London, now sells Rosary Beads, and at Great St Mary's Church, Cambridge, the eucharist is displayed in a gold vessel, and a sign invites people to adore the wafer. The influence of Semi-Pelagian-Arminian teaching about sin and salvation has encouraged a religious humanism "having a form of godliness but denying its power" (II Tim. 3:5). As was the case with Unitarian-Universalist theology, an embrace of Arminianism preceded and prepared the way for a general departure from biblical standards.[42]

Baptists and Methodists

The infiltration and eventual acceptance of Arminianism in the Church of England was not a singular development, for that doctrine appeared among the Baptists early in their history, but the Methodist Church became the only major Protestant denomination to adopt it officially. Baptists originated as an outgrowth of Puritanism-Separatism in England and did not develop from the Anabaptists. During the reign of Elizabeth I (1558-1603), the Church of England was the only expression of Christianity that enjoyed legal standing. Protestants who would not conform sometimes fled to the continent to gain freedom of worship, and the Netherlands was the most receptive country for such dissidents. Communities of English Separatists thus developed on Dutch soil.

One of the early Separatist leaders was John Smyth (c. 1565-1612), a former Anglican pastor, who had renounced Reformed theology before he left England for Holland in 1607. The independent church he organized in Amsterdam became the mother congregation of the English General Baptists, adherents to Arminian teaching, after its leaders disavowed infant baptism. Smyth associated with some Anabaptists whose Semi-Pelagian soteriology he found attractive, and eventually he became a Mennonite. Many members of Smyth's congregation disapproved of his relations with Anabaptists, and under the leadership of Thomas Helwys (c. 1570-1616) that group returned to England despite the hostility of James I (1603-25), the new king, toward nonconformists. Helwys and his followers then founded the first General Baptist Church on English soil at Spitalfields near London. The term *General* signifies subscription to the Arminian view of election and the universal extent of Christ's atonement for all sinners.

General Baptists increased in England in the face of government opposition, and by 1644 they had forty-seven congregations. During the era of Puritan rule (1649-60), Baptists gave much support to Oliver Cromwell and the anti-royalist cause. After the restoration of the monarchy (1660), they endured more persecution, but the Toleration Act of 1689 extended freedom of religion to them and to most other dissenters. The coming of liberty did not, however, bring an increase in spiritual vitality among General Baptists. Instead they drifted into rationalism and Unitarianism, much as Dutch Mennonites were doing at the same time. Although some of their churches resisted this trend, most General Baptists accepted the deviations from orthodoxy. The movement suffered substantial losses to the Quakers, and some whole congregations of Baptists joined the Society of Friends. The Quaker doctrine of the "inner light" as an alternative to the orthodox Christian teaching about human depravity seems to have asserted a strong attraction for the General Baptists, who were already Arminians by persuasion. In the eighteenth century the General Baptists declined to the point that Baptists of today must look to others as their forefathers in early modern history.

In contrast with the Arminian Baptists, who could not withstand the inroads of rationalism, a Calvinistic Baptist movement in England fared better, and modern Baptists derive their origins from this group. Called Particular Baptists because of their adherence to the Reformed doctrines of election and particular redemption (atonement), this movement developed out of an independent Congregational church in London in 1638, when a group of members disavowed infant baptism, and by 1641 insisted upon immersion of believers only. John Spilsbury (1593-1668) led the secession and formed the first Particular Baptist Church in London and remained its pastor until 1656. He was one of the authors of the *First London Confession of Faith* (1644), the first Baptist statement to require immersion. The General Baptists had used pouring as their mode, though they too adopted immersion eventually. Both Baptists and their critics indicated that the practice of immersion began in 1641.

Whereas the General Baptists espoused a Semi-Pelagian-Arminian doctrine of sin and salvation, the Particular Baptists from their inception asserted Reformed theology, as their *First* and *Second London Confession of Faith* (1677) attest. The first Baptist immigrants to America were of the Particular persuasion, and their Philadelphia Baptist Association adopted a slightly modified version of the *Second London Confession*, a statement which is a frank imitation of the Presbyterian *Westminster Confession*. The earliest Baptists in America eagerly aligned themselves with the Reformed faith.

The correspondence between Baptists and Presbyterians is equally clear in the catechisms of the two groups. Baptist leader Benjamin Keach (1640-1704) produced a manual of instruction for which the *Westminster Shorter Catechism* was the model.

The Particular Baptists' adherence to Reformed theology notwithstanding, their influence in England did decline, although it did not vanish. Unlike the General Baptists, the Calvinists responded to the challenge of rationalism with a vigorous defense of their faith. The vigilance with which they guarded the faith was not, however, always beneficial. Some Particular Baptist pastors, in their zeal to uphold Reformed soteriology, drifted into unorthodox teaching now called Hyper-Calvinism: a belief that, since God has predestined the salvation of his elect, the church should not implore people to come to Christ. Without realizing it, advocates of this position were applying a rationalistic method of their own to biblical teaching, and too often Particular Baptist pastors were satisfied to instruct believers while neglecting to evangelize lost sinners. London pastor John Gill (1696-1771) is a fitting example of this harmful procedure. Gill was a scholar of profound ability whose works in systematic and exegetical theology are outstanding,[44] but his conspicuous lack of evangelistic zeal injured both his own ministry and that of less renowned pastors who followed his lead. In contrast to their British brethren, however, Particular Baptists in America participated heartily in efforts to win the lost, so the Baptists flourished there at the same time they were diminishing in England. The effect of Arminianism had sapped the strength of the General Baptists, while Hyper-Calvinism paralyzed the Particular Baptists.[45] It was not long, however, before American Baptists too succumbed to the allure of Semi-Pelagian-Arminian doctrine. In the 1770s, while New York was still a British colony, Free Will Baptists appeared, and traveling preachers spread their teachings rapidly, during an era when revivals of religion were sweeping the country. In 1827 adherents to Arminian principles formed the Free Will

Baptist General Conference, the mother of several agencies that promoted church planting and missions. The traditional Calvinistic Baptists resisted the influx of Free Will teachings for a while, but gradually they relaxed their opposition and tolerated them within their own ranks. Even though some vigorous reassertions of Calvinism occurred among them, the Baptists as a whole drifted from their Reformed foundations, and their *Philadelphia Confession* became only a relic of historical interest. Relatively few Baptists embraced Arminian doctrine overtly, and most of them decried the application of that label to their beliefs. By the late nineteenth century, however, most Baptists in America had adopted a Semi-Pelagian, synergistic understanding of sin and salvation.

Just as England was the birthplace of the Baptist movements, it gave rise to Methodism as well, and Methodists were to exert substantial influence in spreading Arminian ideas, in both England and America. A revival of Christian fervor in Scotland in the eighteenth century soon spread throughout the British Isles, and vigorous preachers formed societies of people who sought a warm-hearted religious experience which they had not found in established churches. Three Anglican clergymen became the most dynamic advocates of revival. They were John Wesley (1703-91), his brother Charles (1707-88), and George Whitefield (1714-70).

While at Oxford University the Wesleys formed a circle of students concerned for their own salvation and to promote godly living. Critics referred to their group as the "Holy Club," and someone nicknamed them *Methodists* to ridicule their actions. Whitefield joined the club in 1735, and his conversion preceded by a few years that of his friends. Whitefield obtained ordination in the Church of England and demonstrated extraordinary effectiveness as a preacher. His view of salvation was that of the Reformed faith. He ministered throughout Britain, wherever he had opportunities, and he did not restrict himself to Anglican pulpits. Whitefield visited America seven times, and the success of his endeavors there was unprecedented, as he united steadfast loyalty to Calvinistic doctrines with zealous evangelism.[46]

The Wesleys too worked in America, in the colony of Georgia, where they arrived in 1735. Although sincere in their efforts to promote Christianity, there was little fruit for their labor and after returning to England they concluded that they were, in spite of their work as missionaries, still unconverted men. Association with some Moravian Brethren aboard ship on their journey to the New World and in Savannah had aroused within them fear for their own souls. After arriving in their homeland, both men sought the company of Moravians in London, and while attending Moravian services, the brothers experienced conversions. On both occasions the writings of Martin Luther were instrumental in bringing the dispirited Anglicans to Christ. While listening to a Moravian at Aldersgate read from Luther's commentary on the Epistle to the Romans, John Wesley, for the first time, grasped and believed in justification through faith alone, and he recorded in his journal, "I did trust in Christ . . . alone for salvation, and an assurance was given me that he had taken away my sins . . . and saved me from the law of sin and death." Charles Wesley had a similar experience, one in which a reading from Luther's commentary of the Epistle to the Galatians was influential.

Although the doctrine of Martin Luther, a vigorous monergist, was decisively important in the conversion of the Wesley brothers, they, in contrast with Whitefield, adopted an Arminian-Semi-Pelagian view of sin and salvation. Disagreements about theology caused Whitefield and the

Wesleys eventually to end their joint ministries, but they separated without acrimony and refrained from criticizing one another. Their associates were not always so generous, and animated disputes between them were common. Whitefield helped to establish a Calvinistic Welsh Methodist Church.

Even though John Wesley always considered himself an Anglican, that church would not accept preachers of Methodist persuasion, and Wesley's scheme to create "societies" of Methodists as adjuncts to Anglican parish churches encountered stiff resistance. Undeterred, the Wesleys established societies throughout the United Kingdom and employed lay preachers as well as ministers in spreading the Methodist message. Some of those preachers were women. By 1787 Methodists realized they could no longer hope for Anglican approval, so they organized a separate church registered with the government as non-Anglican. By then the Methodists were ordaining their own ministers in defiance of the Church of England, which reserved that prerogative for its bishops. In spite of this development, John Wesley still regarded himself a member of the state church and would not admit that a serious rupture had occurred. His brother Charles entertained no such illusion.

Even before the schism from the Church of England became evident, John Wesley sent missionaries to the British colonies in America. Methodist services took place in New York as early as 1766, and Methodist societies were soon operating in Maryland as well. In 1769 Richard Boardman (1738-82) and Joseph Pilmoor (1739-1825) went to America as Wesley's agents, and both of them in turn served St. George's Methodist Church in Philadelphia, which is the oldest Methodist house of worship in continuous use any place in the world.

Boardman and Pilmoor labored in Pennsylvania, New Jersey, and New York, and others carried Methodism to Maryland, Virginia, and the Carolinas, where their energetic preaching excited great interest and won many adherents.

John Wesley deplored the American secession from the British Empire, and the war that accomplished it caused serious problems for Methodists in America. British bishops would not ordain pastors for America, and Wesley held that only ordained ministers could administer the sacraments. In 1784 he therefore ordained two men to go to the United States. This was the step that convinced Charles Wesley that the break with the Church of England was irreparable. Although the Methodists eventually rejected the authority of the Anglican Church, they espoused the Arminian doctrine that was becoming the dominant belief in that body.

In America Methodists were quick to organize a national denomination to supersede the societies they had formed originally. Francis Asbury (1745-1816), whom John Wesley had sent to the New World in 1771, organized a separate Methodist Episcopal Church after the War for Independence, and that body chose him as its first bishop. With Asbury's dynamic leadership, Methodism grew rapidly and became a large, influential denomination that disseminated Arminian principles broadly across the United States. The official Methodist statement of faith became the Twenty-Five Articles of Religion (1784), which John Wesley composed by deleting the Calvinistic portions of the Thirty-Nine Articles of the Church of England. The Methodist articles affirm the sinfulness of human nature and assert that God's grace is essential before lost people can turn to Christ. They do not, however, believe in total depravity, and universal atonement is a prominent emphasis in this statement.

The Twenty-Five Articles are, in general, somewhat vague about soteriology, but the implication is clear that Wesley wanted his preachers to teach that God grants his grace to everyone, and therefore human decision determines salvation. There is no reference to election in this statement of doctrine.[47]

The brevity of the Methodist confession reflects the priority Wesley and other leaders assigned to personal religious experience rather than to precise definitions of Christian doctrine, as a cursory comparison of that document with the Westminster Confession will show. The Wesleyan movement did not reply to the challenge of rationalism with scholarship but presented the testimony of personal experience instead. John Wesley thought arguing with sceptics was futile, so he, in general, ignored the critics of Christianity. His evangelism proceeded on the assumption that salvation is a synergistic matter in which humans have the ability to cooperate with, or to resist, God's grace. As one perceptive interpreter of Wesley wrote, "man is able, not just to resist the grace of God in the Arminian sense of the term, but actually to kill the grace . . . which is already housed within him."[48]

The spread of Semi-Pelagian-Arminian religion from the eastern seaboard of the United States into the western frontier areas was due in large part to Methodist influence. Francis Asbury applied Wesley's program of circuit riding evangelists, and such preachers travelled far to proclaim their message of salvation by human choice, a message rugged self-reliant frontiersmen found attractive. Methodists were the most successful of the denominations working in the new territories west of the Appalachian Mountains, and their conception of Christianity exerted great influence upon other churches which competed with them. Although the other major Protestant bodies did not endorse the Semi-Pelagian-Arminian teachings formally, none of them resisted it entirely, and the laxity in the application of confessional standards allowed synergistic beliefs to become popular, even in churches that still professed allegiance to the Reformed faith.

Modernism, The Consequence of Humanism

The fundamental distinction between biblical Christianity and its numerous competitors is disagreement about the human condition since the fall and the remedy for that condition. The ancient heresies such as Judaizing doctrine, Arianism, and Pelagianism all failed to appreciate sufficiently the impairments which the Fall inflicted upon human nature, especially upon the intellect. To the heretics, denial of such biblical doctrines as salvation by grace alone, the Trinity, and the two natures of Christ seemed to be reasonable responses to rather mysterious concepts. There was a manifest unwillingness to subject reason to the authority of God's revelation, and the underlying cause for this refusal was the heretics' assumption about the autonomy and ultimacy of the intellect and the choices it makes. If humans are mentally and morally competent to judge issues which pertain to God and affect salvation, principles which reason finds deficient must not be true. Historic Christianity, on the other hand, contends the noetic effects of sin have deprived people of the ability to appraise their own limitations, those due to creaturehood and those which result from their fallen, sinful condition.

In the end, the disputes between Christianity and its ancient and modern competitors are reflections of mutually exclusive worldviews. Humanism, whether in its secular or its religious expressions, begins with man and focuses its attention upon his assumed rights and abilities. Christianity, however, begins with God and asserts his sovereign right to reign and rule over all his creatures – those beings who depend upon him for their very existence and must one day give an account to their Creator for what they have done and what they have failed to do. The antithesis between these beliefs is obvious and irreconcilable, although the religious movements examined in this book have tried to synthesize them. Unitarianism and Arminianism have retained some aspects of the biblical doctrine of God while discarding concepts they deemed offensive to reason. The Semi-Pelagian / Arminian view of sin and salvation cites Jesus as the Savior but makes human decision, rather than the grace of Christ, determinative. In this scheme of things Jesus is a Savior who does not actually save.

Modern liberal religion, which calls itself Christian, while rejecting many historical doctrines of the faith, began when Socinus concluded that orthodox theology and Christology were unacceptable because human minds could not comprehend the most profound features of God's self-disclosure. The application of this approach to truth soon led to a broad and deep scepticism across the entire spectrum of Christian belief, and Arminians unwittingly abetted that trend by promoting a man-centred view of salvation. In time, the sites of Arminian strength, for example, the Remonstrant Seminary in Amsterdam and Harvard College in America, became highly influential institutions from which graduates spread Unitarian theology. The collision of worldviews between Christianity and its "competitors" is patently clear in these expressions from spokesmen whose declarations bring the two positions into sharp contrast. As an exponent of God-centred Christianity, the Apostle Paul exclaimed:

161

> *Oh, the depths of the riches both of the wisdom and knowledge of*
> *God! How unsearchable are his judgments and his ways past finding*
> *out. For who has known the mind of the Lord? Or who has become his*
> *counsellor? Or who has first given to him and it shall be repaid to him?*
> *For of him [God] and through him and to him are all things, to whom*
> *be glory forever. Amen (Rom. 11:33-36).*

British poet William Ernest Henley (1849-1903) emphatically stated the humanist point of view in his *Invictus*, a Latin term that means "I have not been conquered."

> *Out of the night that covers me,*
> *Black as the Pit from pole to pole,*
> *I thank whatever gods may be*
> *For my unconquerable soul.*
>
> *In the fell clutch of circumstance*
> *I have not winced nor cried aloud.*
> *Under the bludgeonings of chance*
> *My head is bloody but unbowed.*
>
> *Beyond this place of wrath and tears*
> *Looms but the Horror of the shade,*
> *And yet the menace of the years*
> *Finds, and shall find, me unafraid.*
> *It matters not how strait the gate,*
> *How charged with punishments the scroll,*
> *I am the master of my fate,*
> *I am the captain of my soul.*

Although no one who seriously affirms the Christian faith would concur with Henley's self-centred declaration, those who subscribe to a synergistic understanding of salvation commit the same egregious error by assuming they can make some meritorious contribution by their good works or by the faith they believe they have produced for themselves.

Modern liberalism is the logical consequence of religious humanism, and Pelagius was the forerunner of modernist theologians who reduce Christ to the role of an example and a teacher of fine ethics, while denying that his death atoned for sin and that he rose bodily from the grave. The axioms of modern liberal religious thinkers are the same as those of Pelagius because they assume that human nature is not inherently sinful and that people have the ability to earn God's favour. Liberals insist vehemently that God must not implicate anyone else in Adam's sin and God must grant his grace to everyone, or he would not be fair. Human decision is therefore ultimate in salvation, unless as Universalists contend, no one will be lost under any conditions.

Pelagianism and Semi-Pelagianism, in Roman Catholic and Protestant forms, propound a man-centered worldview which conflicts with the God-centred teaching of the Bible. In the sixteenth century this discord became especially graphic when Erasmus demanded, "God must be good!" Luther responded, "God must be God!" The Prince of the Humanists assumed the prerogative of defining God's goodness for him, while the Protestant theologian maintained that God alone is competent to define his attributes.[49] Luther knew all God does is good because he is the standard of goodness. Pelagianism and Semi-Pelagianism audaciously specify conditions for God, so advocates of those doctrines come under the condemnation of Scripture. The Apostle dealt with accusations that God is not fair by denying that sinful humans have the right to question their Creator and to do so is evidence of their depravity. Humanists demand that God satisfy their standards, but real Christianity holds that creatures must satisfy their Creator, and that he, not they stipulates the terms. The indictment of human arrogance is especially pointed in the Epistle to the Romans:

> *Indeed, O man, who are you to reply against God? Will the thing formed say to him who formed it, "Why have you made me like this?" Does not the potter have power over the clay, from the same lump to make one vessel for honor and another for dishonour? (Rom. 9:20-21).*

Christianity and its competitors are fundamentally exclusive of one another in the most basic principles which comprise their views of God, man, sin and salvation, and their conceptions of reality are irreconcilable.[50]

Note

[1] Tertullian, "A Treatise on the Soul," in *Ante-Nicene Fathers*, III, eds. Alexander Roberts and James Donaldson (Peabody, MA: Hendrickson Publishers, 1994 reprint of 1885 edition), pp. 181-235.

[2] Since only a few of Pelagius' writings have survived, observations of his critics are important sources of information about his teachings. John Ferguson, Pelagius (Cambridge: W. Heffner & Sons, 1956), is a substantial biography. A penetrating analysis of Pelagian doctrine appears in the *Encyclopedia of Biblical, Theological, and Ecclesiastical Literature*, s. v. "Pelagianism," by W. G. Easton.

[3] Despite its age, F. C. Burkitt, *The Religion of the Manichees* (Cambridge: The University Press, 1925) remains a useful source of information, but see S. N. C. Lieu, *Manichaeism in the Later Roman Empire and Medieval China*, (Manchester: The University Press, 1985). An excellent summary appears in the *Encyclopedia of Early Christianity*, s. v. "Mani, Manichaeism," by Pheme Perkins.

[4] Augustine, *The Confessions*, tr. E. B. Pusey (New York: Modern Library, 1949), pp. 188-89.

[5] ibid., p. 158.

[6] ibid., p. 167.

[7] Augustine, "On the Proceedings of Pelagius," in *St. Augustine's Anti-Pelagian Works*, tr., rev., ed. Peter Holmes, Robert Ernest Wallis, & B. B. Warfield in *Nicene and Post-Nicene Fathers*, V, ed. Philip Schaff (Peabody, MA: Hendrickson Publishers, 1995 reprint of 1887 edition), pp. 209-10.

[8] ibid., pp. 436-65.

[9] Helpful studies of Pelagianism and Semi-Pelagianism include J. N. D. Kelly, *Early*

Christian Doctrines, 5ᵗʰ ed. (New York: Harper & Row Publishers, 1978) and Roger E. Olson, *The Story of Christian Theology* (Downers Grove, IL: InterVarsity Press, 1999). The volume of literature about Augustine is enormous. N. R. Needham, ed. has compiled excerpts from the bishop's writings about salvation in *The Triumph of Grace* (London: Grace Publications Trust, 2000). Herbert A. Deane, *The Political and Social Ideas of St. Augustine* (New York: Columbia University Press, 1963), is much more than the title implies and offers a splendid analysis of Augustine's theology as the basis for his worldview. Erudite interpretations of many facets of his thought appear in Roy W. Battenhouse, ed. *A Companion to the Study of St. Augustine* (New York: Oxford University Press, 1955).

[10] See B. B. Warfield, *Calvin and Augustine*, ed. Samuel G. Craig (Philadelphia: Presbyterian & Reformed Publishing Company, 1956).

[11] The text of this papal encyclical appears in Ray C. Petry, ed. *A History of Christianity: Readings in the History of the Early and Medieval Church*, vol. 1 (Englewood Cliffs, NJ: Prentice-Hall, Inc., 1962), pp. 505-06.

[12] *The Canons and Decrees of the Council of Trent*, tr. H. J. Schroeder (Rockford, IL: Tan Books, 1978 reprint of 1941 edition), pp. 31-32.

[13] ibid., p. 34.

[14] ibid.,

[15] ibid., p. 28.

[16] ibid., pp. 43-46.

[17] *The Catechism of the Catholic Church* (New York: Bantam Doubleday Publishing Group for the United States Catholic Conference, 1994).

[18] ibid., #405.

[19] ibid., #403.

[20] ibid., #1731.

[21] ibid., #1738.

[22] ibid., #1471.

[23] ibid., #179.

[24] ibid., #153.

[25] ibid., #161.

[26] ibid., #1996.

[27] ibid., #1993 (emphasis in original).

[28] ibid., #2011 (emphasis mine).

[29] ibid., #2025.

[30] *Westminster Shorter Catechism*, #33.

[31] *Westminster Confession of Faith*, vol. XIII, p. 1.

[32] *The Documents of Vatican II*, ed. Walter M. Abbott, tr. Joseph Gallagher (New York: Guild Press, 1966). See the many references to salvation in the index. The Second Vatican Council did not issue a specific statement about justification and

so did not alter the decision of Trent.

33 *What Luther Says*, II, ed. Ewald M. Plass (St. Louis: Concordia Publishing House, 1966), p. 37.

34 Martin Luther, "The Smalcald Articles (1537)," in *The Book of Concord*, tr. & ed. Theodore G. Tappert, et. al. (Philadelphia: Fortress Press, 1959), article I, p. 292.

35 James G. Manz, *Vatican II, Renewal or Reform?* (St. Louis: Concordia Publishing House, 1966), p. 37.

36 Martin Luther, "Small Catechism" in *Book of Concord*, article III, p. 345.

37 "Augsburg Confession of Faith" in ibid., articles II, IV, V, p. 29-31.

38 For an insightful examination of Anabaptism, see Robert Friedmann, *Theology of Anabaptism* (Scottdale, PA: Herald Press, 1973) and Kenneth R. Davis, *Anabaptism and Asceticism* (Scottdale, PA: Herald Press, 1974).

39 Carl Bangs, *Arminius, a Study in the Dutch Reformation* (Nashville: Abington Press, 1971) is an outstanding biography. For a keen study of Dort and the significance of its decisions, see Thomas Scott, ed. & tr. *The Articles of Dordt* (Harrisonburg, VA: Sprinkle Publications, 1993 reprint of 1841 edition).

40 In 1602 Arminius wrote a rebuttal of a treatise by English Puritan William Perkins which sets forth Arminius' view in detail. The full reply to Perkins is in *The Works of James Arminius*, III, London edition, tr. James & William Nichols (Grand Rapids: Baker Book House, 1991 reprint of 1875 edition), pp. 249-484. The above statement is a paraphrase by Bangs, *Arminius*, p. 221.

41 ibid., p. 258.

42 Interesting accounts of Anglican history and doctrine are Lee Gibbs, *The Middle Way* (Cincinnati: Forward Movement Publications, 1991); Stephen Neill, *Anglicanism*, 4th ed. (Oxford: the University Press, 1977). A vigorous call for a return to the Reformation emphases is James Edward McGoldrick, "Three Principles of Protestantism," *The Banner of Truth*, 233 (1983), pp. 1-12.

44 John Gill, *The Cause of God and Truth* (Grand Rapids: Baker Book House, 1980 reprint of 1855 edition) and his *Body of Divinity* (Grand Rapids: Baker Book House, 1981 reprint of 1839 edition).

45 For a succinct account of Baptist origins, see James Edward McGoldrick, *Baptist Successionism, a Crucial Question in Baptist History* (Lanham, MD: Scarecrow Press, 1994).

46 The best biography of Whitefield is Arnold Dallimore, *George Whitefield* (London: Banner of Truth Trust, 1970).

47 John Wesley, "Twenty-Five Articles of Religion," in Creeds of Christendom III, 6th ed. Philip Schaff, rev., David S. Schaff (Grand Rapids: Baker Book House, 1983 reprint of 1931 edition), 807-13. A fine treatment of Wesley's beliefs is William Ragsdale Cannon, *The Theology of John Wesley* (New York: Abingdon-Cokesbury Press, 1946).

48 Ibid., 114. Reference to Cannon

[49] The debate between Erasmus and Luther on freewill is noteworthy, but 'Humanist' of course did not have the same connotations then: Calvin and other Reformers, are generally seen to have a 'Humanist' approach.

[50] J. Gresham Machen, Christianity and Liberalism (Grand Rapids: William B. Eerdmans Publishing Company, 1946, reprint of 1923 edition).

Chapter Five

GOD'S LAST WORD
THE COMPLETION OF REVELATION

Writing by the inspiration of the Holy Spirit, the Apostle Paul plainly and emphatically affirmed the authority, applicability, and sufficiency of Holy Scripture to make people wise about the matter of salvation obtained through faith in Jesus Christ. The Apostle referred primarily to the Old Testament, since the New Testament was still in the process of composition. It is evident, however, that Paul and other authors of the New Testament were conscious recipients of divine revelation who wrote at the direction of God's Spirit. With full confidence in the Bible he possessed, Paul told his friend and co-laborer Timothy:

All Scripture is God-breathed and is useful for teaching, rebuking, correcting and training in righteousness, so that the man of God may be thoroughly equipped for every good work (II Tim. 3:16-17, NIV).

Paul asserted dogmatically that all Timothy and other

Christians need to know about salvation and living in a God-pleasing manner they will find in Scripture. Could there be a clearer declaration of *sola Scriptura*?

Paul's certitude about the sufficiency of God's written Word parallels the explicit teaching of Jesus on the matter of authority. It is clear that the Savior accepted the Jewish canon of the Old Testament (Luke 24:44), and there is no evidence that he ever cited any other literature as authoritative. Jesus did, however, denounce Jewish teachers who implicitly denied the sufficiency of Scripture by resorting to non-biblical traditions (Matt. 15:1-20).

Although Christ acknowledged the Old Testament as God's Word and based his own ministry upon it, he taught that additional revelation would be forthcoming, as the Holy Spirit came to disclose it. In his own words:

> *I still have many things to say to you, but you cannot bear them now. However, when he, the Spirit of truth, has come, he will guide you into all truth; for he will not speak on his own authority, but whatever he hears he will speak; and he will tell you things to come. He will glorify me, for he will take of what is mine and declare it to you (John 16:12-14).*

Among the disciples the Lord addressed when he promised the coming of the Holy Spirit were future authors of the New Testament. The Spirit of God would teach them about Christ and inspire them to amplify and apply the Savior's doctrine for the benefit of subsequent generations. Because of divine inspiration, the writers of the New Testament claimed to speak for God and thus asserted the divine authority of their own writings.

In the Greek language *exousia* means power and authority over people. One who holds *exousia* may do as he pleases to control people and events. *Exousia* entails power as, for example, exercised by a public official. In secular Greek literature, this term often indicated arrogant use of power, and Jewish critics of Jesus accused him of such arrogance when they asked, "by what authority are you doing these things [miracles], and who gave you this authority?" (Matt. 21:23). On that occasion Jesus refused to comply with the demand to justify his actions, but he later claimed "all authority", that is, full *exousia*, "in heaven and on earth" (Matt. 28:18). Jesus commissioned his disciples to continue his ministry after he ascended to heaven, and he invested them with authority to do so. That is why Paul, for example, stated to members of the church in Corinth "the things which I write to you are the commandments of the Lord" (I Cor. 14:37). When the Lord promised the Holy Spirit would guide the apostles, he "guaranteed the same divine inspiration to the New Testament as he attributed to the Old Testament." [1]

The Bible and the Church

All religious bodies which claim to be Christian profess to accept the inspiration and authority of the Bible in some way. Not all of them, however, subscribe to the sole authority and sufficiency of Scripture in all matters of faith and life. The Roman Catholic Church and the Greek Orthodox Church are clear in their insistence upon extra-biblical authority. As part of their reverence for ecclesiastical tradition, they cite the writings of ancient church Fathers. A careful comparison of the New Testament writers with the Fathers of the church will show that the post-Apostolic authors admitted their inferiority to their New Testament counterparts and did not claim authority over the readers of their treatises, whereas the writers of the New Testament books asserted divine *exousia* and commanded their readers to obey. Polycarp (c. 69-156), Bishop of Smyrna, for example, wrote a letter to Christians in Philippi in which he acknowledged the superior authority of the Apostle Paul. Ignatius of Antioch (d. c. 110), when writing about his anticipated martyrdom, declared "I do not, as Peter and Paul, issue commands to you. They were apostles of Jesus Christ, but I am the very least of believers."[2]

All serious students of Christian history acknowledge the importance of the Church Fathers as sources of information about the ancient church period. It is a mistake, nevertheless, to elevate them to a level of authority comparable to that of the New Testament, as the Roman Catholic and Greek Orthodox churches have done.[3]

Critics of the Protestant doctrine of *sola Scriptura* often argue against it on the basis of their belief that the Bible is the child of the church. This is a serious error, for no action of the church at any point in time made any document Holy Scripture. The church was the recipient, not the validator, of the Bible. There was never a time the Christian Church did not possess a Bible and resort to it as the Word of God. The church depended at first upon the Old Testament, the canon of which had been fixed before the birth of Christ. After the Savior's ascension into heaven, inspired authors wrote the New Testament. Although these writers became leaders of the church, the divine inspiration by which they composed their books occurred before they presented them to the church. There could be no church without the Word of God, to which the church must render obedience and to which it must conform its beliefs and practices. The church is not superior to Scripture but must submit to the written Word.

Opponents of *sola Scriptura* frequently insist that the church exerted decisive authority in selecting the books which became the New Testament. They point to the actions of ancient synods and councils which issued lists of inspired writings. These ecclesiastical assemblies, however, only recognized the books in question as Scripture; they did not make them Scripture. The Holy Spirit inspired the writing of the New Testament documents, and his inspiration alone made them canonical Scripture. John Calvin spoke of this matter with precision when he wrote:

> It is utterly vain . . . to pretend that the power of judging Scripture so lies with the church that its certainty depends upon churchly assent. Thus, while the church receives and gives its seal of approval to the Scriptures, it does not thereby render authentic what is otherwise doubtful or controversial. But because the church recognizes Scripture to be the truth of its own God, as a pious duty it unhesitatingly venerates Scripture. [4]

The official teaching of the Roman Catholic Church regarding the canon of Scripture, it may surprise readers to learn, is more agreeable with Calvin's conclusion than with arguments against *sola Scriptura* now popular within that body. In 1870 Vatican Council I issued a pronouncement which merits quoting at length:

> This supernatural revelation, according to the universal belief of the Church, declared by the sacred Synod of Trent, is contained in the written books and unwritten traditions which have come down to us, having been received by the Apostles from the mouth of Christ himself; or from the Apostles themselves, by the dictation of the Holy Spirit, have been transmitted, as it were, from hand to hand. And these books of the Old and New Testament are to be received as sacred and canonical, in their integrity, with all their parts, as they are enumerated in the decree of the said Council, and are contained in the ancient Latin edition of the Vulgate. These the Church holds to be sacred and canonical, not because, having been carefully composed by mere human industry, they

were afterwards approved by her authority, nor merely because they contain revelation with no mixture of error; but because, having been written by the inspiration of the Holy Ghost, they have God for their author, and have been delivered as such to the Church herself.

And as the things which the holy Synod of Trent decreed for the good of souls concerning the interpretation of Divine Scripture, in order to curb rebellious spirits, have been wrongly explained by some, we, renewing the said decree, declare this to be their sense, that, in matters of faith and morals, appertaining to the building up of Christian doctrine, that is to be held as the true sense of Holy Scripture which our holy Mother Church hath held and holds, to whom it belongs to judge of the true sense and interpretation of Holy Scripture; and therefore that it is permitted to no one to interpret Sacred Scripture contrary to this sense, nor, likewise, contrary to the unanimous consent of the Fathers. [5]

Although Rome officially recognizes the inherent canonicity of the biblical books, it still does not accord Holy Scripture the status of supreme authority. That church continues to extol its traditions, but in the end, it does not allow either Scripture or tradition the place of final authority. That dignity belongs to the church itself. In place of *sola Scriptura* Rome has put *sola ecclesiam* – the church alone, the church as the source of living tradition. The Catechism of the Catholic Church is explicit about this.

The Magisterium of the Church
Question 85. "The task of giving an authentic interpretation of the Word of God, whether in its written form or in the form of Tradition, has been entrusted to the living, teaching office of the Church alone. Its authority in this matter is exercised in the name of Jesus Christ." This means that the task of interpretation has been entrusted to the bishops in communion with the successor of Peter, the Bishop of Rome. Question 86. "Yet this Magisterium is not superior to the Word of God, but is its servant. It teaches only what has been handed on to it. At the divine command and with the help of the Holy Spirit, it listens to this

devotedly, guards it with dedication, and expounds it faithfully. All that it proposes for belief as being divinely revealed is drawn from this single deposit of faith."

Question 87. Mindful of Christ's words to his apostles:"He who hears you hears me," the faithful receive with facility the teachings and directives that their pastors give them in different forms.

The dogmas of the faith
Question 88.The Church's Magisterium exercises the authority it holds from Christ to the fullest extent when it defines dogmas, that is, when it proposes truths contained in divine Revelation or having a necessary connection with them, in a form obliging the Christian people to an irrevocable adherence of faith.[6]

For almost three years (1962-65), Vatican Council II discussed ways to relate traditional Catholic doctrines and practices to the modern world. Some of the council's prouncements indicated major changes in policy, especially as they pertain to relations with other church bodies. No longer would Roman Catholic officials refer to Protestant and Eastern Orthodox churches as heretics, but, in the manner of Pope John XXIII (1958-63), would regard them as separated brethren. The new posture did not, however, signal any substantial change in the teaching of Rome concerning the supreme authority of its own hierarchy. The assertion of ecclesiastical supremacy in the documents of Vatican II is clear and unequivocal. After affirming that both Scripture and tradition are divinely inspired and "to be accepted and venerated with the same . . . devotion and reverence," the council declared:

The task of authentically interpreting the word of God, whether written or handed on [tradition], has been entrusted exclusively to the living teaching office of the Church, whose authority is exercised in the name of Jesus Christ.[7]

This official dogma of the Roman church conflicts with the practice of believers in biblical times who examined the Old Testament to test the claims of Paul and Silas, when those missionaries presented the Gospel in a synagogue of Berea. In a commendatory manner the Acts of the Apostles reports the Bereans "received the message with great eagerness and examined the Scriptures to see if what Paul said was true" (Acts 17:11, NIV). Without any authorization from a religious hierarchy, Berean believers searched the Scriptures, but that is the very practice the Church of Rome reserves for its own teaching magisterium. Although Luke, the human author of Acts, praised the Bereans for their diligent use of God's written Word, Rome appears to say that ordinary Christians are not competent to understand the Word and so must rely on the supposed infallible interpretation of the church.[8]

Moreover, the Roman Church, unrestrained by *sola Scriptura*, has at times issued dogmas that have no biblical basis whatever. This occurred in 1854, when Pope Pius IX (1846-78) proclaimed that the Virgin Mary, "from the . . . moment of her conception, [was] free from all stain of original sin."[9] This dogma, known as the immaculate conception of Mary, not only lacks any scriptural basis, it actually contradicts the New Testament and Mary herself. When the Virgin discussed with her cousin Elizabeth the miraculous pregnancy she was experiencing, Mary responded to a salutation from Elizabeth with the declaration "my soul magnifies the Lord, and my spirit has rejoiced in God my Savior" (Luke 1:46-47). Were Mary without sin, she would not have need a savior. Yet Catholic teaching maintains that Mary was sinless by nature and "remained pure from all personal sin throughout her life."[10]

A more recent example of Catholic willingness to

go beyond Scripture in making dogmatic decrees is the pronouncement of Pope Pius XII (1939-58) in 1950 of the Virgin's bodily assumption into heaven. The catechical explanation states:

> The Immaculate Virgin, preserved from all stain of original sin, when the course of her earthly life was finished, was taken up body and soul into heavenly glory, and exalted by the Lord as Queen over all things, so that she might be the more fully conformed to her Son, the Lord of lords and conqueror of sin and death.[11]

The extravagant claims that Rome makes about the Virgin Mary have not diminished in the post-Vatican II era, while the church has nevertheless tried to improve its relations with separated brethren. The pontiff, John Paul II, in 1987, issued the encyclical *Redemptoris Mater* in which he bestowed lavish praise on the mother of Christ, even to the point of awarding her the divine attribute of omniscience and hailing her participation in the redeeming work of her Son.[12] Such are the lengths to which religious leaders will go when they refuse to be bound by the authority of God's written Word.

All who profess to believe the Scriptures should note carefully how the Word warns its readers against adding to or substracting from its declarations. Moses cautioned the Israelites, "You shall not add to the word which I command you, nor take away from it, that you may keep the commandments of the Lord your God which I command you" (Deuteronomy 4:2; cf. 12:32). The New Testament closes with the stern admonition:

> If anyone adds to these things, God will add to him the plagues that are written in this book; and if anyone takes away from the words of this prophecy, God will take away his part from the Book of Life, from the holy city, and from the things which are written in this book (Rev. 22:18-19).

Although the immediate reference in these passages is to the teaching of Moses and the book of Revelation itself, the principle involved has a wider application. God's people must be content with the revelation he grants them and not resort to extra-biblical means to establish their doctrines or to regulate their lives. The Holy Scripture does not recognize any other inspired authority.

The Finality of Christ

Contentment with God's revelation in Scripture is an expression of the believers' satisfaction with Jesus Christ, the Living Word of God to whom the written Word bears witness. The Bible is a Christocentric book, a fact which Jesus emphasized to the Jews of his day, when he said "you search the Scriptures, for in them you think you have eternal life, and these are they which testify of me" (John 5:39). Christ is the capstone of divine revelation, the Word from God for whose advent the Old Testament was the preparation, as God "spoke in times past to the fathers by the prophets" (Heb. 1:1). The New Testament announces that the One for whom the fathers waited has arrived, and "in these last days [God] has spoken to us by his Son" (Heb. 1:2). The last days comprise the period between the ascension of Christ into heaven and his personal return to earth at the end of history.

As Christians await the climax of the ages, they have in Scripture a sufficient and infallible divine revelation to guide them in all matters of doctrine and godly living (II Timothy 3:14-17). The purpose of God's revelation has been realized in the person and work of his Son, the Savior to whom the incremental disclosures of God's will in the Old Testament bear witness. Jesus Christ is God's supreme self-disclosure, the Word of God incarnate (John 1:1-18). All previous revelation reached its culmination when Christ appeared on earth, and the New Testament is the authoritative record of his life and work and the inspired explanation of his significance. Since there is no other source of information about Christ, it should be evident that divine revelation ceased with completion of the New Testament. There is therefore no reason to expect further communications from God by prophets, tongues, dreams, visions, personal intuitions, or any other means. All God intends for humans to know about his Son is in the Bible.

By adhering to *sola Scriptura*, Christians honor their Savior and the authors his Spirit inspired to write the Bible. Believers thereby affirm their confidence in the trustworthiness of Christ himself. This Christ continually referred to the Scriptures, and he closed his earthly ministry by teaching them to his disciples. "Beginning at Moses and all the prophets, he [Jesus] expounded to them in all the Scriptures the things concerning himself" (Luke 24:27).

Prior to the coming of Christ to earth, divine revelation was expressed in types and shadows as well as in specific predictions. When God became man, however, all shadows vanished, as the incarnation manifested "the light of the knowledge of the glory of God in the face of Jesus Christ" (II Cor. 4:6). Since Christ is the goal and end of God's revelation, and he has completed his redeeming work, the means of revelation are no longer in effect. "As revelation could not be complete before Christ, it could not be incomplete after he came." [13]

Genuine Christianity is biblical Christianity, the bedrock of which is full confidence in the inspiration, authority, and sufficiency of Holy Scripture, as affirmed in almost every Protestant confession of faith since the Reformation of the sixteenth century. When believers resort to extra-biblical means such as ecclesiastical traditions and supposed revelatory experiences to discern the will of God, they implicitly disparage the Scriptures, even though that is not their intention. One of the principal marks which distinguish Christianity from its ancient and modern competitors is and will remain the doctrine of *sola Scriptura*. "The grass withers, the flower fades, but the word of our God stands forever" (Isaiah 40:8).

NOTES

[1] Robert P. Lightner, *The Savior and the Scriptures* (Grand Rapids: Baker Book House, 1978 rpt. Of 1966 ed.), 170. This is a work of exceptional value, one on which the present study has drawn heavily.

[2] *Epistle of Polycarp to the Philippians, in Ante-Nicene Fathers*, I. Eds. Alexander Roberts and James Donaldson, rev. by A. Cleveland Coxe (Peabody, MA: Hendrickson Publishers, 1994 rpt. Of 1855 ed.), 3:21-23, *Epistle of Ignatius to the Romans*, in Ibid., 4:3; Leon Morris, I Believe in Revelation (Grand Rapids: William B. Eerdmans Publishing Company, 1976), 63-64.

[3] The Greek Orthodox Church regards Scripture as the first component of a developing tradition and the writings of the church Fathers as the second instalment. See Timothy Ware, *The Orthodox Church* (Baltimore: Penguin Books, 1963), 203-15.

[4] John Calvin, *Institutes of the Christian Religion*, ed. John T. McNeil, tr. Ford Lewis Battles (Louisville, KY: Westminster/John Knox Press, 1960), I. Vii.2. Calvin's treatment of Scripture as supreme authority is very helpful. See chapters vi-x of Book I in the *Institutes*.

[5] The full text of the Vatican Council decrees appears in Geddes MacGregor, *The Vatican Revolution* (London: Macmillan & Company, 1958). The statement about Scripture is on page 153.

[6] For a thorough, persuasive treatment of this matter, see Sinclair Ferguson, *Scripture and Tradition: the Bible and Tradition in Roman Catholicism, in Sola Scriptura: the Protestant Position on the Bible*, ed. Don Kistler (Morgan, PA: Soli Deo Gloria Publications, 1995), 184-218.

[7] *Documents of Vatican II*, ed., Walter M. Abbott, tr., Joseph Gallagher (New York: Guild Press, 1966), II:9-10.

[8] Excellent analyses of this matter are in *Sola Scriptura*, ed., Kistler. See especially the essays by Robert W. Godfrey and John F. MacArthur.

[9] *Catechism of the Catholic Church*, #491.

[10] Ibid, #508.

[11] Ibid., #966

[12] The text of this document is available on-line at Catholicforum.com. For a keen analysis, see Robert L. Reymond, *The Reformation's Conflict with Rome* (Fearn, Ross-shire, UK: Christian Focus Publications, 2000), 106-9.

[13] For this insight I am indebted to O. Palmer Robertson's *The Final Word: A Biblical Response to the Case for Tongues and Prophecy Today* (Edinburgh: Banner of Truth Trust, 1993), 67. This book is of extraordinary value.

Chapter Six

Appendix: Is the Bible enough?
By Geoffrey Thomas

Our Lord Jesus Christ tells of two men, a rich man who rejects God and a beggar whose trust is in the Lord (Luke 16:19-31). Both of them die, and the beggar goes to heaven, while the rich man goes to hell. One reason he tells this story is so that we may know something of what comes after death. Many will enjoy the pleasures of heaven, but others will suffer the horrors of hell.

This rich man who is suffering the torments of hell makes two requests of Abraham. First, he asks to be relieved of his torment, which is unbearable. But Abraham tells him that that is impossible, saying in effect, "All your lifetime you received your good things; you were reminded of the certainty of death and judgment: you were warned to flee from the wrath to come; you had been told of the mercy and long-suffering of the grace of God; you were told to seek that mercy and find peace through the gospel." But after death it is too late.

The second request of the man in hell deals with his five brothers. They are still in the world, so the man in the pit devises a scheme by which they will not join him there (because their presence, no doubt, would make his hell five times worse). He devises a plan of evangelism – which many human beings do. He imagines a way of delivering his siblings from the place of woe. The five brothers all know the beggar who lived his life at the gate of their rich brother's house, and they all know that he died. So the rich man says to Abraham, "Send that man, Lazarus, from your side back to my brothers to show himself to them as one raised from the dead. The result of that will be that they will become believers, especially when he tells them about hell. If a man should be raised from the dead and tell them what is happening to me, they will change. They will no longer curl their lip and say, 'Nobody ever comes back,' but they will believe in God and escape hell." That is the wisdom of a man in hell. That is his proposal.

That request sparks a debate between Abraham and the man in hell. Abraham argues one side, and the man in hell argues the other. Abraham defends the position of those who believe in God through the Lord Jesus Christ, and the man in hell defends the position of those who use human reason and never trust the Savior in this world or the next. This argument is still going on. It is important for us to see what this argument consists of and the difference between the two approaches.

The Position of Faith
On one side, there is Abraham and all who believe as he did. One thing is true of every one of them: they are satisfied with the Bible. Theologically, we would say that they hold to the

sufficiency of the Scriptures to save any person from hell. Abraham says: "They have Moses and the Prophets; let them hear them: (v.29). Moses wrote the first five books of the Bible. There is Genesis, which tells that God is a personal God, an almighty Lord, and how he made the world, and why the world is in the state it is. It speaks of the great answer to man's rebellion in the Christ who one day will come and bruise the serpent's head. Then, in Exodus, we are told of the Passover, of those for whom a lamb had died substitutionally, and how the angel of death had passed over all of them. Because of the lamb whose blood had been shed, they were forgiven. The book of Leviticus tells us that "without shedding of blood there is no remission of sins" (Heb. 9:22). It points to the sacrifices of redemption instituted by a loving God. The book of Numbers tells us of the brazen serpent lifted up in the wilderness, and that if men obediently look on who and what that represents, they will have life. The book of Deuteronomy tells us of the covenantal relationship between God and his people – Jehovah, the great I Am, pledging himself to be their God and Savior for ever and ever.

"They have Moses," Abraham says, and the rich man's brothers also have the rest of the Old Testament written by the prophets, who together speak of the Lord Jesus Christ. He is there in it all. So Abraham says, "Let them listen to them." How much more should we today listen to those who were eyewitnesses of Jesus' majesty, who were there with him in the upper room, and who heard his cry, "Peace be still!" and saw the waves obey him, and who helped unloose risen Lazarus from his graveclothes. Should we not listen to those who by the Holy Spirit were led into all the truth in what they wrote? Do you see Abraham's argument? The Scriptures are enough to bring a man to faith in Jesus Christ.

The Scriptures themselves are more than sufficient to save a man from hell.

Then Abraham adds, in words to this effect, in verse 31: "If they do not listen to the Bible, nothing else will convince them; nothing else will do any good, not even the spectre of a resurrection before their very eyes." So the question is, Do you agree with Abraham? On one side of the debate, the man in hell says that it seems a great idea to him to send a man back from the grave to the world of the living to warn them (vv. 27-28). But Abraham replies, "They have the Scriptures, let them hear them." "No," the rich man says, "the Bible is not enough." He has no confidence in the Word of God. He is saying, "They need something more than the Bible if they are going to be saved from hell." This man thinks that the Bible is an ineffective book, that you cannot expect anyone to get serious about eternal life and flee from the wrath to come simply by reading the Bible, or by hearing sermons from the Scriptures.

The Position of Unbelief

Now it is very interesting that the man in hell addresses Abraham respectfully and calls him "father Abraham" (v. 24), and that the patriarch acknowledges that and responds to him with the word "son" (v.25). In other words, this man was a fellow Jew – a member of the Old Testament covenant people. He had been circumcised, and ethnically and outwardly he was a son of Abraham. The Lord Jesus in Luke 16 is speaking to fellow countrymen. He is addressing the Pharisees who are sneering at him – "And the Pharisees also, who were covetous, heard all these things: and they derided him" (v. 14 KJV). They could not imagine that they themselves were in any danger of hell. Even when they saw Lazarus raised from the dead, they continued their plotting to kill the Lord Jesus Christ.

This rich man, then, grew up in the synagogue, memorizing the Scripture, hearing it week by week. But he never obeyed it, nor did he love it. He found it boring. He never dreamed for one moment that he would end up in hell. He never thought that one day there would be a great chasm fixed between himself and Abraham. There are many like him who hear the Word of God preached with the Holy Spirit sent down from heaven. Judas heard it; Ananias heard it; Sapphira heard it; Demas heard it; the Judaizers heard it – but all were lost.

Now you see what the rich man is saying from hell – "If the Scriptures are the only thing that you are going to give my brothers, well . . . I had them, and what good did they do me? They didn't change me." In fact, he is saying in hell: "It is perfectly understandable that I didn't believe and that they don't believe – all we had was the Bible. I know my brothers; I am aware of how they live; I know where they are going. The Bible is not going to touch them – men like them need something more." In effect he is saying, "I should be excused. If only I had seen a miracle that thrilled me, I would have believed. If only a man had been raised from the dead and spoken to me, then I would have paid attention. If only I could have gone to a meeting where amazing things happened, it would have been different. But all I had was the Bible. The Bible!"

That is what many people say still. "You can't expect the world to be attracted to the Bible, by preaching the Scriptures, by texts outside chapels, and verses on billboards, and tracts with Scriptures on them, and memorizing the Bible, and lessons from the Bible to children in Sunday school, and camps where young people are taught the Bible, and conferences where the Bible is proclaimed. You can't expect people to be attracted by that! We need concerts! We need drama! We need costumes! We need bands! We need choreography! Bring in the drums and synthesizers. Send in the clowns! Then the people will come. We need superstars and celebrities to give us their testimonies – not just the Bible alone!" But, you see, Abraham was unyielding, "The Bible is sufficient," he said.

Is the Bible enough?

Not a few religious people argue just like that man from hell. The Roman Catholic Church says that the Bible is not enough, that we must have sacred tradition, too. The Quakers say that the Bible is not enough, that there must be an inner voice in the congregation. Modernists say that Scripture itself is not enough, that it must be interpreted by "the assured results of modern criticism." They say that we must go back to the sources "behind" our present gospel narratives to find the "authentic" sayings of Jesus. Cultists say that the Bible is not enough, that men must obey another book – the Book of Mormon, or Science and Health with a Key to the Scriptures, by Mary Baker Eddy, or the Watchtower productions of the Jehovah's Witnesses. Many charismatics say that the Bible is not enough, that it needs to be supplemented by miracles and signs. All such people are saying that the Bible is not enough. They say, "It's a good start, but it needs a bit of help from us."

A preacher has written that when the Apostle Paul was preaching in Athens, he slipped up and as a result few were converted. Paul used wrong methods; he simply preached the Word of God to the philosophers who were gathered there on Mars Hill, and only a few were converted. So Paul went to Corinth and drastically changed his methods. There he performed miracles and many were converted. But the conversion of one of the members of the Greek supreme court named Dionysius, and a woman called Damaris, as well as a number of other people (Acts 17:34) would be considered by us to be very encouraging for the first meeting in a community that had never heard the gospel before. But people are taught that this is not "power evangelism." "Unless we can do miracles, there will be no converts."

"No, father Abraham," says the man in hell, "not the Bible alone - the Bible plus something else. The Bible plus informal entertainment. The Bible plus background music. You choose the "plus." You enthuse about it. You give lectures about it, and write books about it. You can grow rich on it − "How I found the plus that helps the inadequate Bible." You can hold seminars and conferences and tell the world the method that you discovered to compensate for the failure of the Scriptures. You can be like this man in hell who had no love for God, but thought of a way to make up for the inadequacies of the Bible.

Now remember that Abraham was in heaven before Moses wrote the first five books of the Bible. Abraham had a unique perspective on the books of Moses and the Prophets. Abraham was there in the presence of God when the Lord gave the Word to Moses and to the prophets. He was listening to the Lord on those occasions when God commanded the Holy Spirit, the Spirit of illumination, "Go to Moses, Samuel, David, Solomon, Elijah, Isaiah, Jeremiah, and Ezekiel, and assist them to understand my Word, proclaim it, and write the Scriptures, to the very jots and tittles." Abraham heard God speak, and he knew the source and power of that which had come from the throne of the universe. From the lips of the living God had come those words. Abraham knew and loved them: they were Spirit and life. They were powerful words, as effectual as when God had said, "Let there be light" and there was light. The Almighty has broken the silence of the heavens. God has spoken to sinners. He has opened his heart and revealed his inmost Being. He is there and he is not silent. We have his Word.

"God, who at sundry times and in divers manners spake in time past unto the fathers by the prophets, hath in these last days spoken unto us by his Son, whom he hath appointed heir of all things, by whom also he made the worlds" (Heb. 1:1-2 KJV). He is a speaking God, but now in these last days he has spoken to us by his Son – the Lord from heaven, the speaking Savior, the Prophet, God's final Word. The Lord Jesus Christ has said that no one knows the Father except the Son, who alone has that infinite acquaintance. There is the immensity of the Almighty, and only the Son knows him comprehensively. When at the end of his life he is praying, he thanks the Father for all the help that he has had to discharge the commission which the Father gave him. He has omitted nothing, and when Jesus sends his apostles into the world, he gives them the Holy Spirit to lead them into all the truth, and they also omit nothing. Everything has been provided for all that is needed for the over two thousand years of church history. When Paul acknowledges himself as an apostle, he says, "And then last of all to me also" (I Cor. 15:8). In other words, Paul was the last apostle. No more apostles are needed. No house needs more than one solid foundation (Eph. 2:20).

We have Moses, we have the Prophets, we have the Gospels, and we have the Epistles. We have them all in our own English language. We may hold them in our hands, and we can read them. When John Jewel, one of the great English Reformers, who became the bishop of Salisbury, was preaching on the

Scriptures, he ended by rousing his congregation: "Are you a father? Have you children? Read the Scriptures. Are you a king? Read the Scriptures. Are you a minister? Read the Scriptures. Has God blessed you with wealth? Read the Scriptures? Are you a usurer? Read the Scriptures? Are you a fornicator? Read the Scriptures. Are you in adversity? Read the Scriptures. Are you a sinner? Have you offended God? Read the Scriptures. Do you despair of the mercy of God? Read the Scriptures. Are you going out of this life? Read the Scriptures."

Abraham was saying words to this effect: "Do you want your brothers to see a miracle? Your brothers have got a miracle! They have in their hearing at every visit to the synagogue Moses and the Prophets. They may purchase for themselves Moses and the Prophets. They may read and memorize Moses and the Prophets."

We who live twenty centuries later have more, having the Gospels, the Acts, the Letters, and the book of Revelation. These new covenant writings are the miracle which leads the church into the new millennium. When I take this Bible in my hand, I am holding a mighty work of God. I have something absolutely unique. Here is something miraculous in its independence of thought, in the comprehensiveness of its theme, in its utter and invincible confidence that it is the most relevant word to my own life and to that of every man. Sometimes, in moments of doubt, our minds must rest in this: "I have the Bible." I have this great intrusion from heaven, this book that comes from another world in which men may hear the unique utterances of the Son of God. I have read much of human literature at its best, but I find here in this book something that is discontinuous with everything else. Here is a book that is absolutely unique. The Bible is a word from God that knows me, that describes me, that searches me, that finds me. The Scripture speaks to man's deepest needs. Here is a book that contains concepts of unsurpassable grandeur, in words that are invincible in their sheer originality. Every Sunday, when gospel churches meet, they do so around this miracle. Every single service has at its center this miracle – not just those red letter Sundays, when everything is just right. Not merely when the Holy Spirit moves and convicts, but every time we are gathered in the name of the Lord Jesus Christ and this book is in the center of our gathering, then we are meeting in the presence of a miracle. Do you say you want a miracle and then you will believe? Well, here is a miracle! Abraham says "No!" to signs and wonders as the means of saving sinners today, because here is the Bible and it is a miracle. "So then, faith comes by hearing the message, and the message is heard through the word of Christ" (Rom. 10:17).

Abraham knew that this was God's method. So then, you must go to a church where there is a man sent to preach the word of Christ. That has been and always will be the means of saving anyone. Not since the apostolic age has a single person come to faith in Christ through seeing someone raised from the dead, but millions have become believers through hearing the word. Abraham knew that all the children who were there with him in the presence of God had been saved through the Bible, and that the millions more who would join him there would get to heaven in the same way. It was the Scriptures which made them all "wise for salvation through faith which is in Christ Jesus" (2 Tim. 3:15 NKJV). God in mercy has said, "I have as many people coming into the kingdom as the sand on the seashore – they are all going to share heaven with me. They are corrupted rebels. They provoke me dreadfully, but I will forgive their sins, and I will do this for all who believe in Jesus Christ. And this will be my way: by bringing my word to them. I will send them a Christian neighbour. I will put them in a university, and there they will meet witnessing students. I will work through a member of their family, or through the woman who works in that office with them. And I will bring them to a congregation where they will hear the Word of God preached. That is the way I will rescue them from hell. They don't have to be scholars to understand the Scriptures, but I will open their understanding to know the way of salvation through faith in Christ as that is found so plainly in the Bible. "The testimony of the LORD is sure, making wise the simple" (Ps. 19:7 KJV). Ordinary folk can read or hear this message of the gospel and understand it. It tells us that we deserve eternal hell because we are sinners, but that Jesus, because he loved us, died to save us. We have God's message. If men will not listen to it, they will not be convinced even if God should change teeth fillings from amalgam to gold.

The Scriptures are sufficient to make the man of God perfect. How far can the Scriptures take you? They can take you to total maturity, that is, to be "thoroughly equipped for every good work" (2 Tim. 3:17 NKJV). What lies before us? What duties, challenges, and sacrifices will we be called upon to accept? The Bible will completely equip us for them. How can we grow and put away childish things? How can we become mature men and women? How can we become wise? How can we become conformed to the image of Christ? Through the Bible – that is God's way. The Scripture sanctifies and perfects what is imperfect. It thoroughly enables us for the challenge of every good work in whatever God asks us to do. Every mountain God asks us to climb, every burden he asks us to bear, every service he asks us to give, every pressure he asks us to endure, every sacrifice he asks us to make – the Scriptures can enable us to do it all by preparing us comprehensively for every good work. They tell us how to do it and why we should do it; they give us strength for the task and warn us how not to do it. The Scriptures will complete that good work which God has begun in us. The Bible helps us to put away childish things. The Bible saves a man from being a wimp and delivers him from being a nerd. It transforms him into being "a man of God . . . thoroughly equipped for every good work" (2 Tim. 3:17 NKJV). It is a supernatural blessing to have the Bible.

Our Lord Jesus Christ ends the Sermon on the Mount by speaking about a wise man who built his house upon a rock. And the storms, winds, and floods came, and the house still stood. That man was building his life on the teaching of the Lord Jesus Christ and it stood. Christ was looking forward down the centuries, even looking into the hideous modern era in which we have lived for so long. Christ knew all the storms that would be hurled at little Christian boys or girls; the gales of scientific pretension, of philosophy and humanism, of materialism and fleshliness. Yet every young Christian who stands on the teaching of Jesus will survive any storm. The Savior is absolutely confident about it.

The professing church is in a hopeless, demoralized state whenever its members begin to believe that the Bible is insufficient for the task before us. The Roman Catholic Church, the Quakers, the modernists, the cults, and the charismatics are all looking for some additional signs and voices. None of them is in a healthy state. None of them is convinced about the sufficiency of God's truth. The issue confronting you is, are you content with the Bible or not?

The author is the pastor of Alfred Place Baptist Church in Aberystwyth, Wales. Unless otherwise indicated, he provides his own translations.

Suggestions for Further Reading

In addition to the items mentioned in the notes, all of the following works are valuable for obtaining a deeper, clearer understanding of the issues with which this book deals.

The Authority of Scripture

Bruce, F.F. *The Canon of Scripture*. Downers Grove, IL: InterVarsity Press, 1988.

Chantry, Walter. *Signs of the Apostles*. Edinburgh: The Banner of Truth Trust, 1973.

Ferguson, Sinclair B. *Discovering God's Will*. Edinburgh: The Banner of Truth Trust, 1982.

Geldenhuys, J. Norval. *Supreme Authority*. Grand Rapids: William B. Eerdmans Publishing Company, 1953.

Harris, R. Laird. *The Inspiration and Canonicity of the Bible*. Grand Rapids: Zondervan Publishing House, 1971.

Henry, Carl F. H., ed. *Revelation and the Bible*. Grand Rapids: Baker Book House, 1958.

Lloyd-Jones, M. *Authority*. Edinburgh: The Banner of Truth Trust, 1985 reprint of 1958 edition.

Marston, George W. *The Voice of Authority*. Philadelphia: Presbyterian & Reformed Publishing Company, 1960.

Stonehouse, Ned B. & Paul Woolley, eds. *The Infallible Word*. Philadelphia: The Presbyterian Guardian Publishing Corporation, 1946.

Warfield, Benjamin B. *The Inspiration and Authority of the Bible*. Philadelphia: Presbyterian & Reformed Publishing Company, 1948.

Weeks, Noel. *The Sufficiency of Scripture*. Edinburgh: The Banner of Truth Trust, 1988.

Young, Edward J. *Thy Word Is Truth*. Grand Rapids: William B. Eerdmans Publishing Company, 1957.

The Person and Work of Jesus Christ:

Blanchard, John. *Meet the Real Jesus*. Darlington, UK: Evangelical Press, 1989.

Morris, Leon. *The Lord from Heaven*. Grand Rapids: William B. Eerdmans Publishing Company, 1858.

Olycott, Stuart. *Jesus Is Both God and Man*. Darlington, UK: Evangelical Press, 2000.

Pipa, Joseph A., Jr. *The Root and Branch*. Philadelphia: Great Commission Publications, 1989.

Robinson, William Childs. *Our Lord: an Affirmation of the Deity of Christ*. Grand Rapids: William B. Eerdmans Publishing Company, 1949.

Salvation:

Blanchard, John. *Right with God*. Edinburgh: The Banner of Truth Trust, 1971.

Hodge, Charles. *Justification by Faith Alone*, ed., John W. Robbins. Hobbs, NM: Trinity Foundation, 1995.

Kuyper, Abraham. *Particular Grace: a Defense of God's Sovereignty in Salvation*, tr., Marvin Kamps. Grandville, MI: Reformed Free Publishing Association, 2001.

Warfield, Benjamin B. *The Plan of Salvation*. Grand Rapids: William B. Eerdmans Publishing Company, 1955.

Wells, Tom. *Faith, the Gift of God*. Edinburgh: The Banner of Truth Trust, 1983.

Cults:

Allan, John. *Shopping for a God: Fringe Religions Today*: Grand Rapids: Baker Book House, 1987 reprint of 1986 edition.

Jenkins, Philip. *Mystics and Messiahs: Cults and New Religions in American History*. Oxford: the University Press, 2000.

Lewis, Gordon R. *The Bible, the Christian, and the Latter Day Saints*. Phillipsburg, NJ: Presbyterian and Reformed

Publishing Company, 1966.

Ludlow, Daniel H., ed. *The Encyclopedia of Mormonism, 5 vols*. New York: Macmillan Publishing Company, 1992.

Martin, Walter R. *The Kingdom of the Cults*, rev. ed., Minneapolis: Bethany House Publishers, 1985.

Martin, Walter R. & Norman H. Klann. *Jehovah of the Watchtower*. New York: Bible Truth Publishing Society, 1953.

Ostling, Richard H. & Joan K. *Mormon America*. San Francisco: Harper Collins Publishers, 1999.

Penton, James M. *Apocalypse Delayed: the Story of Jehovah's Witnesses*. Toronto: the University Press, 1985.

Van Baalen, Jan Karel. *The Chaos of the Cults, 5th ed*. Grand Rapids: William B. Eerdmans Publishing Company, 1967.

About the Author

After twenty-eight years on the Faculty of Cedarville University in Ohio, James Edward McGoldrick became professor of church history at Greenville Presbyterian Theological Seminary in Taylors, SC. He received the B.S. and M.A. degrees from Temple University and the Ph.D. from West Virginia University. McGoldrick's special interest in research and writing is the history of Christianity, particularly the era of the Protestant Reformation. He is the author of Luther's *English Connection* (1979), Luther's *Scottish Connection* (1989), *Baptist Successionism* (1994), and *God's Renaissance Man: the Life and Work of Abraham Kuyper* (2000), the last a publication of Evangelical Press. His articles have appeared in such periodicals as *Modern Age*, *Sixteenth Century Journal*, *Calvin Theological Journal*, *Westminster Theological Journal*, *Reformation and Revival*, and *Banner of Truth*, and he had contributed to *Great Lives from History*, *Historical Dictionary of Late Medieval England*, *Historical Dictionary of Tudor England*, *Dictionary of*

Scottish Church History and Theology, *Oxford Encyclopedia of the Reformation*, and *New Dictionary of National Biography*.

Index

Christian Focus Publications
publishes books for all ages

Our mission statement —

STAYING FAITHFUL
In dependence upon God we seek to help make His infallible Word, the Bible, relevant. Our aim is to ensure that the Lord Jesus Christ is presented as the only hope to obtain forgiveness of sin, live a useful life and look forward to heaven with Him.

REACHING OUT
Christ's last command requires us to reach out to our world with His gospel. We seek to help fulfill that by publishing books that point people towards Jesus and help them develop a Christ-like maturity. We aim to equip all levels of readers for life, work, ministry and mission.

Books in our adult range are published in three imprints.

Christian Focus contains popular works including biographies, commentaries, basic doctrine and Christian living. Our children's books are also published in this imprint.

Mentor focuses on books written at a level suitable for Bible College and seminary students, pastors, and other serious readers. The imprint includes commentaries, doctrinal studies, examination of current issues and church history.

Christian Heritage contains classic writings from the past.

Christian Focus Publications, Ltd
Geanies House, Fearn,
Ross-shire, IV20 1TW, Scotland, United Kingdom
info@christianfocus.com